THE
Darlinda Story

THE Darlinda Story

RITA DAVIDSON

With a foreword by
Elaine C Smith

M & A THOMSON
1990

The publishers would like to thank the following for their assistance and for their kind permission to reproduce copyright photographs:

The Barrhead and Neilston Historical Association   page 18
Randolph Caughie   page 115
Old Paisley Society   page 18
Scottish Daily Record and Sunday Mail Ltd.   pages iv, 33, 48, 52, 74, 107, 112, 121
St. Andrews University and Valentine's Archives   page 25

Artwork prepared by Dorothy Hamilton (pages 185, 188, 190) and William Docherty (pages 149–172).

Cover Artwork by *Iain Love Graphics*.

Printed in Great Britain by
M & A Thomson Litho Ltd., East Kilbride.

ISBN 0 9513963 1 5

CONTENTS

FOREWORD

WHEN someone asks an actor what he does for a living and the actor tells the truth (rather than say he's a plumber!) he is apt to be met with a chuckle and a 'Yes, but what's your real job?' The same must be true of a clairvoyant or an astrologer—unless of course you are Darlinda! Darlinda is most certainly a 'star' amongst those who have the ability to see into the future—you only have to try to get an appointment to find that the bookings are full for the next year! Not only is she well known though, she is also highly respected which is a great plaudit for anyone in her line of work and it is due not only to Darlinda's warm personality and everyday attitude to what she does, but also to her hard work, her amazing ability and the accuracy of her predictions.

The world in which we now live does not value highly enough these skills and abilities that Darlinda possesses. To practice them you are viewed as a bit of a freak and to go for a reading you are seen as being a bit daft!

When I was asked to write this I had doubts as to how I would be viewed, but then I felt that I had to do it because of the remarkable things Darlinda has told me over the years and the fact that I do believe that hers are valuable abilities. This book will demonstrate just how many people feel the same—sceptical at first but eventually convinced.

It's all to do, I think, with a caution in our society about dealing with anything new or different—a very basic fear. But we should be relieved to know that these skills exist throughout the world and have done for hundreds of years. Neither church nor state has done much to alleviate that fear in all of us. Instead they've played upon it and done little to encourage people to embrace other senses in the truly spiritual side of our lives.

It seems a great pity that a part of the human spirit and mind has to be closed off and termed 'the bogeyman' and that we're told that only one way is correct. To my mind, that attitude is the kind that starts wars against other races or religions or creeds, and that must be wrong.

It also appears that this is a very 'male' or 'macho' fear about anything a bit unknown, yet men also have a pleasant fascination for it, too. Most now would shy away from it, yet those who have encountered it openly have been amazed and convinced by it. It was a man who first told me to visit Darlinda and there are many excellent male clairvoyants around, too. However, women seem to embrace it much more as a part of life and are prepared to accept it willingly as a skill—maybe that's something inherent, I can't say, but certainly the ordinary working-class women that surrounded me while I was growing up had all consulted a 'fortune teller' at least once.

I believe we all have this special skill of Darlinda's to some extent. We have all entered a room and experienced peculiar feelings of being there before, or been aware of a strange atmosphere there. Or perhaps we've met someone who gives us the creeps or disturbs us for no apparent reason. In this world of ours we rarely use this extra sense—though I do feel that the nineties will see us using it in a more constructive way. As human beings we are more than intellect and body—we are spirits too.

Darlinda is someone who has this gift. She is a fine example of someone who has a highly developed 'sixth sense' and she puts it to great use and for this should be congratulated and applauded.

Hopefully this book will do all of that.

ELAINE C SMITH

Chapter 1
NOW, LET ME SEE . . .

MRS M—'s hands shook as she shuffled the Tarot cards for me. She was about twenty-five, smartly dressed, and obviously very, very nervous.

She cut the pack into three and I dealt out the spread on the low table between us. The cards fell in a particular way which told me she was at a crossroads in her life.

'You're thinking about breaking a family tie,' I said. 'From your husband, possibly.'

The next card, the two of pentacles, virtually confirmed this. A new man would come into her life. The ten of pentacles . . . she would be moving into a house with someone else.

The Empress was prominent. A pregnancy? The six of pentacles meant that she had money problems and did not know what to do about them. But she should not panic as her financial state would get better. Again the sign of a pregnancy, and this time I had to warn her that the father might not be her husband.

The pattern of cards sent out sign after sign. There would be obstacles as well as changes. She would have to gamble with her life to get what she wanted, but it would be hard to know what was best to do. A man would help. Her father, probably. There were indications of a journey which she would wonder whether to take. 'Take it,' I said.

I looked at the final card. Her husband's health. Some trouble. Could be self-inflicted.

I leant back in my chair. 'That's the first part,' I announced, as cheerily as I felt the occasion called for. She seemed to relax a little, and held out her palm to me without any hesitation.

1

She had a long life-line, and three small lines next to the marriage line. 'Oops!' I said silently to myself. Clearly she was going to have three marriages, or else two marriages and an affair with a third man. I told her this. I could see lots of happiness ahead, and some travel too. The lines also showed that she had had a bad time lately. 'Watch out for nerves and depression,' I advised.

Then I sensed rather than felt a tiny vibration and had a curious feeling of her taking off a ring. 'Careful you don't lose a ring,' was what I said.

Someone with the initial 'D' was going to be upset by something she said or did and she would get annoyed at this. There would be an illness in the family too.

'There's a man coming into your life,' I went on, without looking up at her. 'Very soon. You'll be happy with him and you'll laugh together from the word go, though you'll not be too sure of him at first. There's no sign of any illness for you, but watch out for an ankle. You could twist it or something.'

Sensations were buzzing round me now, and I spoke faster and faster to keep up with them.

'You're on an emotional roundabout. Don't know where to get off. Possessions—you don't know what's yours, what isn't. Your husband is in the same state. You've got worries but they'll go. Money is coming, perhaps a legacy. Not for a wee while though.'

I sat back again and looked at her. 'Want to go on?'

She was smiling now. 'Please,' she said.

I put my crystal ball on her upturned palm and told her to wish. Actually it is not a crystal ball but a large glass paperweight. Looking through it helps me to concentrate.

Up from behind the ball and into it came a strong initial 'B', with a wishbone going round it. I told her it represented a male and he was not feeling too well or satisfied at the moment. He had a headache and something was wrong with his chest or stomach. Then I saw a child, one very important to her—a clever child too. There would be a separation, but only temporary. The child would also have some mouth or throat trouble.

Then came a sense of broken or shattered glass. That spelt emotional trouble. Home problems too. A change of house was coming, however, and much sooner than expected.

'In fact,' I said, 'you'll see quite a few houses before you make up your mind on one. I can see you going upstairs in another house that you'll visit to see if you'd like to live there, but you won't stay there permanently. There's a church too. You'll go into it. It's big, beautiful, with stained glass windows. You're looking up at them—blue, yellow, absolutely gorgeous. You'll take up another religion too, and you'll have to do a lot of reading up on it.'

At this point I felt strong psychic vibrations coming from the ball—blue ones, going round and round and pulling me in like a whirlpool. Then they stopped, as suddenly as they had come.

I told the girl that the tenth of next month would be significant and she would get a letter that she did not seem to be very pleased about. Not that it was a bad letter. She was just frowning while she read it. And I saw her walking into a place like an art gallery. There were colours all round her and lots of things would happen to her there.

There was a wishbone at the centre of the ball, and a star of hope shone above it. 'You'll get your wish too,' I said, 'but not exactly in the way you expect.'

I had finished. 'That's it, then, unless you want to ask me anything.'

She looked at me curiously. 'I don't think so . . . You see, you've already answered my question. Except . . . ,' she stopped and looked down at the ring on her wedding finger, 'can you tell me if I'll leave him this year?'

I took up the Tarot pack and told her to pick any seven cards. I laid them out. The most prominent were the two of cups and the four of wands. . . .

Mrs M—'s husband (his name turned out to be Bernard, by the way!) *did* become ill, and in a way his sickness was self-inflicted in that it was traced to the bouts of depression which he suffered as a result, frankly, of his own blunders. At the same time she was already looking around for a new home for herself though the right house had not yet turned up.

She did meet a man to whom she was immediately attracted. The relationship brought happiness at first, but then depression set in caused by emotional indecision. When I last saw her she hadn't yet got pregnant, but, to quote her own words, 'It must have been a close thing. And twice I certainly thought I was.'

It *was* her father who helped her through the tough emotional times that I had predicted. A cousin died and, much to Mrs M—'s surprise, left her some money. The tenth of the next month brought a letter from her bank manager! And her Uncle David got upset about her decision to break her marriage ties.

The child was her daughter who the next day fell and cut her lip. To complete the chapter of accidents Mrs M—, running downstairs to pick her up, twisted her ankle and knocked a stone out of the ring she was wearing. She had to take the ring off and give it to the jeweller to be repaired. She was wearing that one because she had just lost her engagement ring, though happily that turned up a few weeks later. After these and other excitements she was tempted to get away for a few days, but wondered whether she ought to. Then she remembered my advice about a journey, and took one, feeling all the better for it afterwards.

The most surprising prediction, she confessed, had been the one about her changing her religion. However one result of her emotional confusion had been the need to return to religion and when last seen she was thinking of being converted to a different faith.

Mr D— was slim, bespectacled, athletic-looking, and clearly determined to give nothing away during the interview. There was also a hint of scepticism about the way he shuffled the Tarot cards and cut them decisively into three separate piles.

The Hierophant was the significator, and I could see also that my client was going to look afresh at his life very soon. As the picture unfolded I forgot everything but the pattern of cards on the low table between us and what they meant. As I do when this happens, I began to speak fast and very much in a monotone.

'There'll be changes . . . soon . . . and an illness—perhaps someone in your house or family. A holiday . . . will do you good. A lady . . . good advice about money. A change of home . . . quite soon.'

At this point he obviously could not keep up his taciturn attitude. I heard a small, half-stifled chuckle, though whether of astonishment or disbelief I could not tell. Nor, to be honest, did I care. I took no notice and pressed on with the cards.

Good cards came up—the nine and ten of cups, but with them was a suggestion that he should not expect too much from business that year. There would be decisions to take over the next twelve months which would involve spadework for plans much farther in the future. The position of the nine of cups indicated that he could suffer from too much drinking. The six of pentacles, taken in conjunction with the cards around it, showed that he would be thinking of ways to save money. Indeed more than anything else money seemed at that time to dominate his life, but the signs were good as there were a lot of cup and pentacle cards on the table.

'You'll reap what you sow,' I pronounced in conclusion. 'The more you put into getting what you want, the more success you'll have.'

Then I took his hand to read his palm. Apart from that small involuntary outburst earlier on he had remained impassive, and I could feel from his hand that he was in some way trying to stop any vibrations that might be there from passing to mine.

'You'll have stomach trouble,' I said. (There did not seem any point in beating about the bush.) 'But a long life. There's also some trouble up here. . . .' I put my left hand up to my chest while I waited for the picture to clear. 'Heart, I think. . . . But not for years yet. Problems with your teeth too. . . .' About this I was absolutely certain, as I was myself suddenly getting a sensation of my teeth being sore. 'There's someone with a 'W' . . . talking to you. Don't trust them completely.'

The tree of prosperity was clearly marked in his hand, but I had to add that his own prosperity would need to come with the help of someone else. The initial 'T' was prominent, and clearly would have great significance over the next few months. Someone in his family, perhaps his father, would have trouble with his chest. The letter 'A' showed up, and this could be the first or second initial of that person's name. He would also shortly be talking to a policeman or a lawyer about something of importance.

I placed the crystal on his palm. As I did so, I sensed a lessening of tension in him. His hand was steady, and I concentrated my mind down to a pinpoint of light in the ball's interior. After a bit I saw him signing a document. A lease, it could be. A lawyer or a bank manager was handing him the paper and on it were three signatures.

'Important letter... in a long white envelope. It'll come within a seven. Before that... a telephone call that'll alter your way of life. That'll be within a three. It seems to be about a house that you'll go and see. White, Georgian-looking... trellis-work in the front.'

The letters 'P' and 'B' were coming through now. 'B is talking to you about the house,' I said, 'but don't believe automatically everything he says....'

There was much else, but these are the things I really remember about this man's reading. The vividness was acute. So much so that as he got up to go I had no feelings of disappointment when his reserve at last broke and he said, 'Not bad.... But that business about the house... sheer rubbish. Sorry.' And he turned and walked quickly from my room, through the outer office and down into the street.

When he left my office it appears that Mr D— had no intention whatsoever of buying a new house. For one thing he could not afford to. Three days later a friend rang and persuaded him (just for the outing) to go with him to look at some new houses. Mr D— was so impressed by them that he put in an offer for one. (The extra outlay later proved to be justified as his wife's business chose that moment to prosper.)

His new house was white, built in Georgian style, and had a trellis-work fence in front. It was built by a firm whose name begins with 'B'. 'W' was the initial of the name of the site representative. The name of the road in which it stands begins with 'P'. 'T' is for the mortgage company that loaned the money, and the sale document Mr D—'s lawyer handed him to sign already contained three signatures.

Mr D—'s father is called Allan, and he did contract some chest complaint. And Mr D— himself had to have a tooth extracted shortly after his interview with me.

The lady from Fife was small and slimly-built, with every outward sign of being cheery. But when she sat down opposite me I felt waves of depression flow across to me.

There was nothing unusual in the Tarot reading, no real hint as to what was the cause of her unhappiness or whether it would be dispelled. This is one reason why I use several methods of prediction in one reading. Often vibrations come through more strongly with one than with another.

So it was in this case. Her palm showed me clearly that someone close to her had been very ill. I saw too that she would be married twice, and I realised that the illness had been to her first husband and that he had recently died. And she was to be a grandmother shortly, for the first time.

As I explained all this there was no outward reaction from her. But when I sat back to take up the crystal, she looked at me and smiled. A little smile, belying the sadness in her eyes.

'Yes,' she said quietly, 'it's nice about the baby, isn't it?'

The images in the crystal were of a translucent clarity which is rare with most subjects.

'Robert,' I said. 'That's his first name. The man you'll marry next. Surname beginning with 'M'. Tall, well-dressed, with his own business. He'll be driving a brown car when you meet him first.'

It's difficult for a recently widowed woman to be told she will remarry. All sorts of guilt feelings come into play. But that is what I saw and that is what I told her.

'But . . . I don't *know* anyone like that,' she protested. And then as though to get off the subject. 'Do you see anything else?'

I saw travel, lots of it, and change—change all for the better. And happiness again. With these rather less radical predictions her self-composure returned and the veneer of cheeriness reinstated itself.

'You were so right about the present,' she said as she left. 'But I'm sure I don't know about the rest. . . .'

One day, some time later, the lady's daughter and son-in-law took her to a local night-club. Sitting across the room on his own was a tall, well-groomed man whose face seemed familiar from her early life but whose name she could not recall. When he got up to go, the daughter followed a few steps behind. A few minutes later she was back, all agog.

'He's got a *brown* car, Mum,' she said, and subsided giggling into her seat.

The lady from Fife says she did not know at this point whether to laugh out loud or lapse into stunned silence. Instead she did neither. She made some discreet enquiries at the reception desk.

'Yes, madam,' she was told, 'that's Mr Martin. Mr Robert Martin.'

She returned shakily to her seat. 'I'm going to marry that man,' she announced.

Her family, who had been taking the whole thing as a joke, thought she was off her head. But she went out socialising in circles in which Robert might move, and sure enough one day she saw him. She introduced herself and the relationship blossomed from there. He was a widower, and four months later they were married. Since then they have travelled widely—indeed when she came to tell me her news, they were just back from a holiday in Miami.

———————

There was an air of respectability about Mr S—, and an expression of seriousness on his face mixed with faint embarrassment. I sat him down, and began to deal the Tarot.

The first card to come out was the Fool. Then the Chariot. Obviously he was going through a difficult time.

'It's decisions, decisions, at the moment . . . ones you've made or are going to make in the next few days. Maybe they're the most important of your life. There's something in your past life which has caught up with you, and you could be paying for it now. But if you've got determination' (I was choosing my words carefully) 'and think hard before deciding anything, you'll see it through all right.'

I went on, 'There's a problem with a male member of your family. You'll need to take him aside and talk to him about it, get him to conform to certain standards. . . .'

His business prospects certainly looked bright. A new opportunity was in the offing which would prove, if he took it, very successful. The final card in the spread was the eight of wands.

'That's travel,' I explained, 'connected with your business—but you may have to change your lifestyle to manage it. The sign of Aquarius is prominent in the spread—someone under that sign will come into your life soon and play a big part in your affairs.'

I asked for his palm and he didn't seem very keen at first. It turned out to be one of the clearest I have read.

His life was in two parts—one cycle due to finish at that very time, to give way to the new, and better one. The cause of the change would, however, be something rather unpleasant. There was a woman too—she was the most important thing to him but, if he wasn't careful, he'd lose her.

'You aren't as well-off as you used to be.' There was a slight grunt—he was bending to me more now. 'But things will improve in that direction—maybe better than before.' Slightly louder grunt. Of relief, this time.

Other lines and signs confirmed the message of the Tarot—opportunity and success in business, travel. . . . There was a letter too, which he would get within a nine, and which he'd find difficult to understand—but that would be the writer's intention.

I put the crystal on his palm, the back of his hand flat on the table. I gathered my concentration. 'You're sitting with your head down . . . alone. You look as though you're ashamed of something you've done.' The hand that held the crystal wavered momentarily. 'But not to worry too much . . . it's in the open now and it'll soon be forgotten. And there's someone with the initial 'C' in this too. . . .'

The images came fast now, blurring each other, and I had to wait until one separated from another. There was a lucky four. Animals, and a home in the country surrounded by them. A close friend or member of his family was in trouble with the law and he, my client, was getting him out of it. He would later join a society for helping unfortunates. And politics too . . . they'd play a part in his life later on.

The hand had not wavered again. I could feel a strength, physical as well as of purpose, gradually taking hold.

He shook my hand as he left. 'Thanks a lot,' he said. 'And I *mean* that. . . .' He turned to go, then hesitated.

'You know . . . the name I gave you isn't my real name.'
Then he was gone.

I was not surprised in the slightest. . . .

The interview with Mr S—certainly suggested to me a
hint of the kind of scandal some newspapers, and their
readers, appear to relish. It might have made a good
reading, if I knew what actually happened. As it is, he has
never come back, and I have no idea who he was. Nor
have I any interest in finding out.

There was something unusual about the girl who came to
my office one day—something that felt false. When she
sat down my concentration was immediately attracted to
the wedding-ring on her hand. 'Why are you wearing that
ring? It's not yours,' I said. Nor was it. She confessed she
had borrowed it for the interview from a friend who was
waiting outside for her. I suggested she take it off, give it
back, and that we'd then start again.

Only the other day a very correct and polite lady, on
holiday from England, came for a 1.30 p.m. appointment
(I remember that we had fitted her in because there had
been a cancellation—normally I seem to be booked up
one year ahead and currently have a list of 400 people
waiting for cancellations). Towards the end of the interview I glanced up at her and said, 'I can hear scissors
clipping and there are bits of hair falling on my face.'

'Heavens,' she said, looking at her watch, 'I forgot.
I'm having my hair done at two o'clock!'

I am psychic. It is as simple, but sometimes as complicated, as that. Without any warning I will come out with, 'It'll be a boy,' to a girl who doesn't even know yet that she is pregnant, or to a man whose wife is pregnant but has not told anyone but him about it. 'I hope you'll enjoy your trip to New York,' I once said to someone I'd only met seconds before, when he'd only just been told, and in 'strictest confidence,' by his boss that he was to go.

One morning, in September 1978, I was standing with my daughter at home looking out of the window. I heard bells ringing and I suddenly found myself saying, 'The Pope is dead.' At that time John Paul I had been Pope for little longer than three weeks. Yet, only a few days after that, he was dead.

I feel things and know them to be true, even if I don't know why or how I feel them. And I have to say them.

Chapter 2
A STRANGELY HAPPY
CHILDHOOD

W HEN did you first realise you were psychic? This
is often one of the first questions I am asked
when meeting someone for the first time. The
answer to this question is that it wasn't me that realised it
to begin with, it was my family.

I was the seventh child of a seventh daughter. My
mother, Bridget Breslin, was the seventh daughter born
in a family of thirteen. She gave birth to seven children.
My oldest sister Helena came first, then came my brother William, who died in Canada nine years ago. My sister
Morag came next, then my mother had a stillborn boy
whom she had intended to call Harry or Henry after my

My family was a happy one (I'm the beribboned one at the front).

father. Margaret Mary was the fifthborn. Then, sadly, my mother gave birth to another stillborn boy, again to have been called after my father. Seventh in line, I arrived, much to my father's disappointment as he deeply yearned for his name to be carried on. My mother asked him to register me as Anne Elizabeth but after a few whiskies he was determined the name should be Henrietta Teresa. (Until now the only people who knew what H. T. Davidson stands for were the Inland Revenue and the Voters Roll!)

My family couldn't bear to call me Henrietta so my name became Baby Breslin and that name stuck until the night before I went to school. Baby Breslin was not a name to start school with! A hurried decision was made—my name became 'Rita'.

The family home was a happy one which centred on my mother. She was a wonderful Sagittarian who was saintly and who took a great interest in everything that was going on. She loved fun and music and was delighted when one of my sisters or my brother would play the piano and the whole family would join in the singing. Most evenings some friends would drop by and a concert would ensue. Every one of my sisters and my brother could play the piano well. I went along to piano lessons every Saturday morning for about two years but the piano is definitely not my forte. However I do love all sorts of music and music still plays a very important role in my life.

I was the odd one out in the family, having no singing voice at all. This didn't stop me trying. I once played guitar in a group based in Paisley called the Stitch Dime Skiffle Group. Although I could play the guitar quite well they dropped me after about six months as they just couldn't bear to hear me screeching! My family were more forgiving and we had lots of fun on long winter nights with a coal fire blazing and family and friends clustered around the piano in our living room.

When I started school at the age of five, I began at the local primary school, St. John's. However, my mother decided that I should have a better education than my elder sisters and brother so, at the age of seven, I joined St. Margaret's school in Paisley which was posh and fee-paying. I can't honestly say that I ever really enjoyed school—I was a bit of a rebel. I had a perfectly good brain but wouldn't use it. I hated authority and strict discipline. I also hated snobs and there were plenty of them around. It seemed to me at that time that the more money the family had the more attention the pupil got, which I thought to be terribly unfair. My three sisters had all gone through the secondary part of St. Margaret's school before me and they were all quite clever so the nuns expected great things from me and were disappointed with my results, especially after all their efforts in pushing me through exams.

I can remember travelling to St. Margaret's primary school on a rickety old tram car. I went with my sister Margaret Mary who was in the secondary school at that time. (The fare was $1\frac{1}{2}$ old pence—I can't remember if that was the single fare or return!) I can clearly recall getting strange feelings about people and I would sit and gaze at their auras. (An aura is an area of colour around a person, the colour denoting character-type and state of health.)

I remember seeing a dark mottled aura around a girl with whom we travelled. Her name was Christine. This aura worried me for ages and I remember feeling quite sick at times when thinking of her. I was devastated, but not altogether surprised, when one morning at school we were told that she had died. She had been absent from school for just a month. She had died of leukaemia.

When I joined St. Margaret's Secondary School, I travelled every day with the daughters of one of the local

St. John's School, Barrhead.

St. Margaret's School, Paisley.

school teachers, Maureen and Anne Guy. We became close friends and remained in this happy union for many years. We were all in the school hockey team, so Saturday mornings would be a busy time with either our home games at Paisley or venturing on the train to visit the other schools in the league. I usually ended up having black and blue marks on my legs. I was always quite wicked on the field and my opponents usually managed to get their own back!

Sports days at school were a bit of an exciting non-event for me as I was never a Liz McColgan but envied everyone who was fast off the mark. I was in the yellow team called St. Theresa's. The St. Philomena's team wore a blue band. One night about a year ago my friends Anna and Marie brought a friend, Anne, round for supper. I thought I had never met the newcomer who is the wife of a well-known Glasgow lawyer. No one mentioned the school I had gone to in Paisley but all of a sudden I said to Anne, 'You went to St. Margaret's and you wore a blue sports band.' Anne had, indeed, been several years ahead of me at school and as I looked at her I could see her in her school days wearing the coloured band.

As I have said, my mother was a seventh daughter and I was her seventh child. The psychic gift I have, I got from her. Late on in her life (she was forty-five when I was born) she never needed to phone me if she needed some help. She would 'will' me (as she put it) to phone *her*. This is a facility I now have myself. A great way to save on phone bills, as you can imagine!

Unfortunately, I never had such a close relationship with my father. Perhaps because he so wanted a son and I represented the dashing of his last hope. I could never fulfil his requirements. He died from a heart attack when I was seventeen. I suffered in our relationship because I always knew how my father felt about me.

By contrast my mother and I were always very close, and this was probably strengthened by the fact that when I was young we were often on our own together, with no younger brothers or sisters requiring her constant attention. We'd sit by the fire for hours watching the patterns of the flames and the shapes that the soot made when it

Me and my friends, Maureen and Ann, and Laddie.

fell, and she would tell me what these things meant. For example, one day we saw a lady dancing in the flames and my mother explained that we'd be invited to a big party or a wedding. And so we were!

Another time she might say 'That looks like a male visitor with a hat on.' In a short space of time, sure enough, there would be a man standing on our doorstep wearing a hat. Perhaps she would say 'Oh look, there is an invitation coming to one of the girls to go to a dance', and we would both look at the dancers with lovely dresses, dancing about in the flames. The phone would ring within a short period and there would be great excitement when Helena or Morag had to make a dress or perhaps alter one which was second-hand. Everyone helped in the effort to make the lucky one the Belle of the Ball.

As a child of three or four years old, I can remember occasions when I felt as though I was sitting under an umbrella of doom and despair. I could never describe to anyone why I was feeling so down and eventually I would just cry. I often made the excuse of having tooth-ache. Before long the household would hear of a neighbour or relative dying or perhaps of an accident or the radio would bring news of a world disaster. I had 'sensed' a tragedy before it had happened. On the other hand, I would occasionally be in a happy mood for no obvious reason, would feel that my father would be lucky that particular night at the greyhound racing. Lo and behold he would come in the door with a big smile on his face having won several hundred pounds. On a similar level (and perhaps more useful-ly) the telephone would ring and I would be able to say who the caller was before the receiver had been lifted. These events happened so often that my family gradually came to the conclusion that I had a rather special gift.

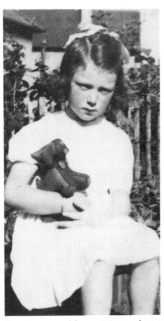

Here I am, aged four, sitting under an umbrella of doom and despair as you can see!

I remember when I was told that my only brother, Bill, had been called up to join the army. I was three or four and I can vividly remember the letter coming in and my mother crying because her wee boy had to go away and wear a uniform. He was eighteen and he was taken to Basingstoke in England. Unfortunately the damp conditions led to him going down with pleurisy. My mother always insisted that he would have died at this time if it hadn't been for the Salvation Army who managed to keep him warm and feed him. He dropped into the Salvation Army hostel and soup kitchen one day and happened to mention that he was a family friend of the top lady at the Barrhead branch of the Salvation Army, a Mrs. Cochrane. That was his passport to hot food and an extra blanket.

When Bill was away my mother would take a cup of tea and make sure there were plenty of tea leaves at the bottom of the cup. From it we would find out how Bill was getting on. I remember her saying things like 'there's a lot of grey water, must be some trouble going on around him.' Sometimes she would see the sun shining on a long leaf near the top of the cup. This was an indicator that there was a letter on its way. The initial B for Bill or W for William would often be present and she would then look all around for some indication of what was going on; for instance a sword would mean news of his health. Often her assessments were spot on. When I stared into the tea leaves I could point out things that she had missed. Often I could hear voices giving me messages but it was all a bit garbled at the time. After four months in the army my brother was discharged as his health had deteriorated rapidly and he was sent home to my mother's open arms and good wholesome food. He hated eggs but she thought they were good for him so she baked two into sponge cakes for him every day.

This unusual mode of communication with my brother continued all through our lives. When, much later, Bill, who was a restless Gemini, decided to go to Canada my poor mum was broken-hearted once again. His girlfriend Frances had emigrated the year before and when he told the family that he was going to join her I can still hear the whole family crying as the realisation gradually dawned that he was going very nearly to the other side of the world and we might never see him again. No-one was ever allowed to utter the word 'Canada' at any time before the dreaded day of departure came along. We all went down to Greenock at an early hour one morning to see him boarding the tender which took him out to the big liner that was anchored further out in the Clyde. My mother was a nervous wreck until she got news of his safe arrival. Some time later I developed a strange pain in my back. As I hadn't been doing any unusual exercises I wondered why I was in pain. It was a sore and strange pain. The next day word came from Montreal that my brother had been in a car accident and that he was in hospital with a fractured spine.

A friend of my mother's, Molly McGuire, visited us from America when I was about six. This lady had worked with my mother in the Neilston Mill when they were both fourteen. She had subsequently emigrated to the United States and had made her mark there reading playing cards and tea leaves. Everyone was astounded when she looked at my teacup and exclaimed that I would one day be a world famous clairvoyant.

I had mixed feelings about this as the only people I had ever seen doing this kind of thing were fairground gypsies with crystal balls. I quite liked the idea of being famous and the gold earrings had a certain appeal but I definitely didn't want to live in a caravan and wear a scarf on my hair all the time. I don't remember much about my psychic powers at school. Perhaps I kept quiet about them in order not to be thought of as odd. I do recall children remarking often that I seemed to know all their secrets without being told!

Apart from these early indications of an unusual psychic power, I don't think my childhood was any different from that of my friends. I loved stories and when I was little my mother would read me stories just like every other child. My favourite story was *Peter Pan* but I could never understand why the big dog called Hanna was locked outside in a kennel and wasn't allowed in the house. This really upset me and I would sob for hours. Another story I cried over was one about pit ponies who stayed underground until they were really old and when at last they were taken up to ground level they were totally blind. I still feel sad when I think of those poor ponies.

Holidays for me were no different than for all the other children who lived round about. We all went 'doon the water for the fair'. The usual destination was Rothesay where the world and his wife appeared to own a room and kitchen. There was always a great deal of excitement especially when the room and kitchen was bulging at the seams with assorted relations. These included my Aunt Maggie, an Aquarian spinster who loved all the little luxuries that money could buy. Also my cousins from Clydebank—there were eleven in the family but I'm glad to say they didn't come on holiday all at the same time! Out of that family my cousin Irene was nearest my age and she was my best friend.

As soon as we opened our eyes in the morning there was a wonderful smell of sliced sausage being fried by my mother and it didn't take long for a queue to have formed for her sausage filled rolls. Never again in life did rolls with sausage taste as good as those Rothesay ones did—definitely a Rothesay delicacy. The seagulls on the island appeared to be twice the size of seagulls in any other place. Our older cousins would tell us stories of birds carrying wee girls away to their nests. The boat to Rothesay wasn't what I expected. I had imagined the liners which I had seen pictures of: the ones that went to America. I have had a lifelong ambition to go to America and have never fulfilled it. When I went to Canada I went as far as the border near Niagara Falls but I still didn't set foot on the other side. On three different occasions I have been booked to go and have had to cancel at the last minute. I wonder what waits for me in this forbidden country?

Rothesay, as I remember it then.

I always remember the echoes of Rothesay public baths. This frightened me. At that time I felt that people who were in another world were trying to contact me. I was too young to understand. One particular day I saw a man with a dark suit on, diving into the water; I screamed and everyone said I was making it up but it was so clear to me.

I remember once when I was about fourteen I was walking up Barrhead Main Street and I met a man who was a friend of my father, Mr Murphy. I was going to the post office to post some newspapers to my brother in Canada and I told Mr Murphy where I was going. He asked me how my brother was getting on and then told me about some chest pains he had been having and that he was going to the hospital in Paisley the next day to have an examination. The time I met Mr Murphy was about 4.30 p.m.—it was after I had come home from school. When I went home I told my mother about the meeting and she in turn told my father when he came home. Later in the evening Mr Murphy's daughter phoned to say her father had been taken to the Paisley hospital with chest pains that afternoon about 3.30 p.m. and had died in the hospital at 4.30 p.m.

Several things similar to this have happened in my life and they always make me feel uneasy and gloomy. I remember feeling really down and grey one day when I was about seven and I couldn't get my mood lifted no matter what I tried. Later in the evening a young lady's face kept coming into my mind. I could smell gas. I told my mum about this and she checked our gas cooker but it was fine. In a short time a neighbour came running to the door with news of another neighbour. A young lady in her twenties had taken her own life by putting her head in an unlit gas cooker. This horrible thought has been with me ever since that black day.

Childhood family outings seemed very exciting although we didn't usually go very far. Our old car would get packed up with all sorts of interesting objects. A folding table, deck chairs, an old kettle, a Primus stove which had seen better days, an assortment of rugs, heavy cardigans and rain coats. My mum and sisters stood for hours making up sandwiches and baking wee buns and cakes.

Even the old dog, Laddie, was squeezed into the car which was bulging at the seams. The destination was usually the local reservoirs, or dams as they were locally known. My father and brother would meet up with the other anglers and stories would be told about how big the fish was that they nearly caught. My Uncle Willie and Aunt May would come along with the family and I would play for hours with my cousin Tessa while all the gossiping went on and the tea was made—far days from jumping in the car and meeting a friend for lunch in the *Rogano*.

In my twenties my next door neighbours were Anne and Jackie Young. Anne is still one of my closest friends. My mother used to say that Anne could wash blankets, go to Dalry, paint a house, dig the garden and make a dumpling all in the one day. I'm sure there was slight exaggeration in this statement but Anne can certainly manage more than most people: at the moment she is building a new kitchen! She was always at the end of a phone when I needed her help while on dialysis. I'm sure Anne could have been a brilliant engineer or electrician. In fact she is a Jack of all trades and master of most!

Some of my first friends in life were the children of neighbours, and Sadie and Ellen remained my friends for years. We would usually end up playing in the Cowan Park where I still walk my dogs nearly every morning. It looks the very same except that some rhododendron bushes near the putting green have now disappeared. I used to think the park stretched for miles and that it would be impossible to walk around it in one day. I now complete the course in fifteen minutes so it's only a fraction of the size it appeared to be when I was a child. I remember one day a chute (or slide) was erected and it had been treated with something to slow us down. We soon learned that if we got the waxed paper that the Co-op bread had been wrapped in and sat on it we could really fly down the chute . . . and straight off the end, to crash land, bottom first. Needless to say, there were a lot of sore bottoms next day! Like in every other park, there were always queues of would-be Wimbledon finalists waiting at the tennis courts. I was as keen as the next child but I never quite made the semi-finals of the local tournament, never mind Wimbledon. Ice skating at Paisley ice-rink was another of my hobbies during childhood. I remember one wonderful Christmas morning when, to my surprise, Santa Claus had left me a pair of new, white skating boots. They were a wonderful luxury compared to the tatty old ice boots that I had been hiring from the rink for years. My sister Helena soon made me a nice skating skirt which my mum insisted shouldn't be too short as it was sinful to wear a skirt too far above the knees. I soon found a way of twisting the waistband over and over to raise the hemline. I must have been a pretty sight trying to play the part of an international ice skating star at Paisley ice-rink with a thick belt of skirt bunched round my waist!

I was a keen supporter of the Paisley Pirates which was the local ice hockey team. My brother-in-law Shaun used to take me to support them most Friday nights. It was so exciting collecting all the autographs of the 'big stars'. There weren't many of them so the autographs were repeated over and over again.

During the long summer break from school I was always wanting to go somewhere. The annual holiday to

Rothesay came and went too fast. My poor mother always tried to please everyone so at my request she would take me to my Aunt Ellen's in Clydebank, and leave me there for a week. It was great fun leaving Barrhead with my small suitcase and tennis racket. At the age of nine I imagined Clydebank to be in another country altogether. The bus would take us to Paisley Cross and then we continued on another bus to Renfrew where the old ferry would take us across the river Clyde to Yoker (I always thought this a strange name for a place—it sounded like a town in Japan). We would then catch the Parkhall bus that would take us to my holiday resort in Clydebank. My Aunt Ellen was a Scorpio who was as busy as a bee looking after her husband, Pat, her seven daughters and two sons. No matter how many she had sitting around the dinner table there was always room for one or two more. My cousins did everything with such style and flair: they always had a box of crisps in the corner of the kitchen—this was really the big time as far as I was concerned! Two of the older girls May and Margaret had gone to America as G.I. brides. There was a cutting from an old weekly newspaper, framed and hanging on a bedroom wall: the by-line read 'Orange groves for Margaret'. The second oldest of my cousins had married a man who owned an orange grove. This stirred my imagination no end; it was like something I had once seen in a film at the Pavilion picture house at Barrhead. There was a photograph of Anna, the fourth oldest girl, on the mantelpiece of the bedroom I slept in. She wore a black piece of ribbon around her neck with a small brooch adorning it and her hair was swept up at the back and sides. I tried to get this look for years after. My hair would never stay in position the way hers did, nor would the ribbon around my neck stay intact. Aunt Ellen was a wonderful cook, the vegetable soup she made had a wonderful aroma, but I have never liked leeks and it was quite difficult to avoid the leeks while supping it. After the soup and the main course she always had home baked cakes. She was famed for her Albert cakes and Victoria biscuits.

My mother would leave me in Clydebank and return home to look after my father and her own family. I generally stayed for a week. I was usually quite happy until mid-week and then I would start to miss home very much. I would sheepishly phone home with all sorts of excuses to leave and be delighted when my mother would arrange to take me home the next Saturday. My Clydebank cousins had a big influence on my life. I thought they were part of a set from Hollywood. One of the sons, John, was in the Merchant Navy and the house was full of trinkets and pictures from all over the world. It was in that household that I tasted my first prawns—now they are a favourite part of my diet.

I have never been a good baker although I have tried time and time again. I remember once when I was about ten my mother decided that I should learn to make pancakes. She helped me to get the right amounts of the right ingredients and mix it until I got the right texture. She showed me how to cook one side then flip the pancake over to brown the other side. In a short time I became very adventurous and, trying to be smart (and make life more interesting), I flipped a large pancake high in the air. My father's good white shirt had been ironed and was airing on the pulley above the cooker. He was to attend a major greyhound race meeting straight after work. He allowed himself half an hour to eat his dinner (which of course would be placed on the table as soon as my mother saw him turning the corner) wash and change. So what happened to the pancake? It flew into the air and hit the gleaming white, perfectly pressed shirt, sticky-side to shirt, of course. In those days my father only had one white shirt. I ended up hiding in a wardrobe fearfully listening to my father shouting while my mother tried to save me by telling a white lie about his good shirt having been stolen off the rope in the back green. This may have been the incident that blighted my chances of becoming a baker. Who knows what deep psychological effects it may have had? Well, that's my excuse anyway!

I was to become well acquainted with hospitals in my life but my first encounter with a hospital was when I was nine. My sister Morag had been suffering on and off for years from a quinsy throat, and our doctor eventually sent her to see a specialist at the Victoria Infirmary in Glasgow. The specialist was of the opinion that the tonsils should be removed as soon as possible but unfortunately there was a two-year waiting list for the operation. The family decided that it must be done privately so Morag was admitted the following Monday for the operation. She was really ill and I remember my mother asking everyone to pray for her.

She came home, quite well, ten days later. The bill for her stay in the private wing of the Victoria was £22. A considerable sum in those days. Today the £22 would probably just cover the price of a bunch of flowers to brighten the patient's bedside!

When I was ten my sister Helena gave birth to my first nephew, Denis, who was a whizz kid from a very early age. He knew the words of many songs when he was just two years old and wherever he went Denis was asked to sing. He loved the limelight! One night when he went along to a concert in the Nitshill Hall to hear the local choir singing he waited until the choir were braced, just ready to render a rousing verse and he sung it out before they did. Everyone just fell about the place laughing—choir included. Denis has gone on to become a priest, with a fine voice for leading the singing. He frequently appears on TV and radio so we're almost a media family now!

Chapter 3
MAKING MYSELF USEFUL

I LEFT school at the age of fifteen with few qualifications, in spite of the nuns' endeavours. I decided to
train to be a florist which suited me well as I have an
artistic flair. I started out in Cashmore's, the florist, in
Paisley and graduated to Toni Gilmour's, situated right
in the centre of Glasgow. One day, in that shop, while I
was concentrating on making up a wreath, twisting flowers into a wire frame, the wreath suddenly appeared to
me to burst into flames and I saw men wearing uniforms
falling into the flames. I was terribly upset and caused
quite a commotion in the shop. That evening, 28 March
1960, nineteen firemen and men of the Glasgow Salvage
Corps

The Cheapside Street Fire.

died fighting a fire in a whisky bond in Cheapside Street, Glasgow. A few days later I stood helping to make up wreaths for those killed that night. I cried for days afterwards. This was my first experience of this kind, and it was horrific.

It was about that time that I met George, the man I would later marry. He was keen on astronomy, but sceptical about astrology and clairvoyance!

Also at about this time, I had a terrible nightmare which I remember vividly to this day. I dreamed someone was sticking hypodermic needles into me. I thought about this constantly the next day and then told my family and George that I thought I was going to get diabetes. If any of them believed me, they certainly did not show it. One year later, diabetes was indeed diagnosed.

In fact, I had had typical symptoms of the disease for some time. I remember having an unquenchable thirst—I could never get enough liquid to drink. I drank bottle after bottle of lemonade or milk and when all that ran out I just stood beside a water tap. Of course I had to find a loo every place I went. I got thinner and thinner until I eventually weighed less than seven stone. I was like a walking skeleton.

One Sunday evening I was so ill that my family called in an emergency doctor who made the grim diagnosis and ordered an ambulance to take me to Belvidere Hospital in the east end of Glasgow. I remember parts of the ambulance journey through the city. I was in a state of confusion but I can still hear the sirens making a clear passageway for the vehicle. I remember a young doctor meeting the ambulance and giving me my first of what were to be thousands of insulin injections. The massive dose of insulin which was needed to lower my blood sugar made it drop too quickly and I was then verging on a hypoglycaemic coma. I lay in a bed for several days wondering if I would make it or not. I also wondered how I could possibly manage to inject myself—no this was not for me. Why me anyway? Had God stopped loving me? Several days passed. Then I was given an orange and a syringe and shown how to administer an injection. I cried for the poor wee orange as I shoved this big needle into it. I felt very vulnerable but I was also very strong willed. The doc-

My sister, Margaret Mary, and I, in our Sunday best!

tors and nurses in the hospital were super: so patient and tolerant! One minute I accepted that I would have to inject myself for the rest of my life and the next minute I didn't want to know about it. By the time I was discharged from hospital, however, I had made up my mind that if I had to live with diabetes, diabetes was going to have to live with me and it wasn't going to hold me back from doing anything I had planned to do.

After I had accepted the fact that my diabetes was here to stay, I began to wonder if anyone else in the family had ever suffered from it. So I asked my mother. She thought not but later I discovered that my grandmother, who was in her eighties when she died, had had an unquenchable thirst and the doctor had put her on a diet of chicken and brown bread. She also went blind before she died—this can be a side effect of diabetes. She died in 1920, the same year that Banting and Best discovered insulin in Canada. My mother didn't know at that time that her son, Bill, had developed diabetes in Canada three years before. He had kept this a secret from our mother as he knew that she would only worry about it. When he heard that I was diabetic too, he sent me a telegram of consolation and broke the news to the family that he was a fellow sufferer.

My poor mother! I gave her a terrible shock myself once! Not long after I became diabetic, she tried to wake me one morning and found to her horror, that I was profoundly unconscious. I was in a deep hypoglycaemic coma caused by having a surplus of insulin in my blood.

I was 'rushed' to hospital in an ambulance. It was a dreary, foggy, damp day and visibility was poor so the journey to the Victoria Infirmary took three times as long as it would normally have done. The ambulance was involved in a minor crash at Shawlands Cross and my mother was thrown on to the floor and suffered a bruised face and leg. Apparently we were both admitted to different parts of the casualty department for treatment! I don't actually recall any of this as I was still in a coma at the time.

When I regained consciousness the first question I asked the doctor who had been injecting glucose into my arm was 'Am I dead?' I had imagined I had been hurtling backwards through a long black tunnel like a vortex lined with black bricks. I was very reluctantly being forced against my will. Try as I might I couldn't stop myself being sucked through the vortex although I knew I didn't want to reach whatever was at the other end. I was really glad when the doctor confirmed I was indeed alive. I could not be disposed of that easily—I still had a lot of damage to do as the old saying goes.

I was twenty-one when I married George, a Cancerian and a lovely person but, as it later turned out, not the right one for me. (We realised after a number of years that we were quite incompatible and decided to part amicably, as amicably as any divorce can be.) However, at first all was well, we happily set up house together and, despite my diabetes, we soon decided to start a family.

Gary, my first child, was born in Blackpool Victoria Hospital. After he was born, by caesarian section, I was told that he had been born with hyaline membranes in his lungs and he didn't have much chance of survival. This is a common condition in babies newborn to diabetic mothers. As I was too ill to be moved, the nurses brought his incubator to my bedside and I remember looking at this tiny, gorgeous baby boy and begging him to live—tears dropping onto the incubator. He must have got my message, or perhaps it was all the prayers that were said that did the trick, but I left hospital two weeks later with Gary in my arms. I thought God must love me again and I said a big thank you to Him.

Five years after Gary was born I became pregnant again. I was advised to have the pregnancy terminated as I was told that I had been lucky the first time but would probably not be so lucky the second. I was determined to have the baby but I had to spend four months in hospital during the pregnancy. When Selina was born in Glasgow Royal Maternity Hospital she weighed only five pounds and once again the delivery was by caesarian section. Again I was asked not to hold out too much hope for her survival. When I saw her in an incubator she appeared to have tubes going into, and coming out of, every part of her tiny body. But she got stronger every day and was allowed to leave with me after two weeks. I couldn't wait to see the dainty doll of a baby in a lovely wee dress. When she was six weeks old I went back to work again— my family complete.

Around the time of Gary's birth my psychic powers seemed to become much stronger. I would just happen to mention something to a friend and within days, or

37

sometimes hours, that particular thing would happen. For example I remember dreaming that Clark Gable would die and the next day, sadly, he did die.

George regarded things like teacup reading and Tarot as definitely weird. I admit that at that time I only read teacups myself for a giggle, but one day he asked me, with an indulgent smile, to do it for him. As I peered into the cup trying to make sense of the pattern of the leaves I saw something quite different from anything I'd seen in a teacup before—an image, as though through glass, of George kneeling beside a couch on which a woman was lying. There was a huge initial O above her. A small cross on the wall behind her suggested to me that she was dead.

The name of George's mother was Olive. I said, 'We've got to go and see your mother . . . now.' When I told him what I had seen in his cup he agreed (at least in part to humour me) that we should go up straightaway. The house was unusually still as we approached it. He rang the bell. There was no answer—nor any sound at all from the house within. George got up on to a window ledge and looked into the living room. His mother was lying back on the couch, motionless. Even before he forced his way in through the window, we knew that she was dead.

Once when I was a patient in the Southern General Hospital I got the strange feeling that the lady in the next bed was going to die. When my visitors came up that evening I reluctantly told them of my fears. They took them seriously enough as such fears had been shown to be justified on many occasions before. When the night sister came on duty she enquired why I wasn't asleep, the time being around midnight, and I told her of my worry. She tried to reassure me by saying that the woman was quite well and would be discharged in a couple of days' time. Still not sleeping by 2 a.m., I was given a sleeping pill by the doctor on call, after the sister had relayed my fear to him. Before falling asleep I could hear what sounded like a cart rattling along on cobblestones outside. I knew this was quite impossible as outside there was only a broad lawn and then the motorway leading into the Clyde Tunnel, not a cobblestone in sight! At the same time as this was happening I could hear the echo of voices chanting *The Angel of Death*. Minutes later the patients were rudely woken by the sound of a defibrillator being rushed into the ward—the forty-year-old lady's heart had stopped beating. Tragically, it did not re-start. Doctors and nurses later came from all parts of the hospital to view this funny psychic lady who had known what was going to happen. This type of experience was becoming more and more of an everyday occurrence.

One Sunday afternoon my friend and I had been invited out to another friend's house for lunch. I had never been in her house before. On the Saturday night I had had a strange dream: I was standing in a room with lots and lots of old ornaments all around me, lots of pictures on the walls, and piles of books on the floor. At the end of the room there was a big pine bookcase and it was empty. My friend's father said to me 'Rita, go pick up all those books, and put them into that bookcase. They shouldn't be lying all over the floor.' The next day we went to lunch and were introduced to a couple we had never met before. The couple said they knew my friend's father and they chatted about him. When we eventually entered the front room there were piles of bric-a-brac and ornaments lying around the place and before I could sit down I had to lift books off the chair and place them on top of another pile on the floor. I looked around the room and found the big pine bookcase standing against one wall, empty.

One evening my friend June and I were sitting discussing a gentleman who had temporarily gone out of her life and gone to Spain for a while. We were talking in great detail about him when all of a sudden a big plate bearing the word 'Spain' fell from the wall and smashed into a hundred pieces on the floor.

I am unable to explain events such as these. Of one thing I am certain: they do happen, and really quite often.

My mother always appeared to know when something was going on that concerned one of our family or a close friend. I was the only one in the family who understood her feelings, the truth being that I usually had the same feelings—we had a strange way of sharing feelings.

Often we would have similar dreams on the same night. On one November morning in 1967 we were sitting having a coffee and I was thinking of the strange dream that had troubled my sleep. I had dreamed that children were trying to swim in mucky water and when I dream of dirty water, something nasty usually happens. My mother cut into my thoughts telling me about the dream she had had of small children getting immersed in mud and being unable to get out of it. Shortly after 9.00 a.m. that day, an 800 ft colliery slag tip at Aberfan, Glamorgan, slipped and engulfed a primary school, a row of terraced cottages and a farm. By lunch time that day the news was being broadcast of the awful disaster in a small town in Wales, where the final, dreadful death toll was eighty one.

Sometimes my mother and I would share a similar dream that was nice and foretold something good. One night, in June 1962, we had a similar dream about fields of flowers and one of us identified them as larkspur. Next day, sure enough, a horse called Larkspur won the Derby and came in at 22:1. I wish these kinds of dreams would occur more often but unfortunately they don't. I'll never make my fortune that way.

I am frequently asked whether my two children are

psychic or not. Both Gary and Selina can sense if something is wrong with me and are in touch shortly after something happens. Selina and I often have the same sort of dreams on the same night, just as my mother and I used to do. One day Selina and I discussed what we would buy our old friend Nan for her birthday; Selina decided on a toilet bag and some nice soap and I decided on underwear, so we went our separate ways to purchase the gifts. In the evening we showed one another our purchases and looked at each other in bewilderment when we both produced exactly the same umbrella, bought in two different branches of the same store! Selina is always disappointed when I can guess what she has bought me for my birthday!

At Christmas Gary had been going out with Lesley for about nine months but insisted he wasn't getting married until he was thirty. He enjoyed the freedom of his bachelor days. A few days before Christmas, Selina was quizzing him over lunch as to what he was buying Lesley for her Christmas present and he said it was a surprise. He was the surprised one when I suddenly said, 'It's a four stone, diamond engagement ring, bought from a shop in Renfield Street.' Gary nearly fell off his chair but he still didn't admit I was correct—until Christmas morning!

Poor Gary! Sometimes my psychic gifts cause him problems in more ways than one although it's some years now since he came home from school trying unsuccessfully to hide a black eye so loud that it looked as though it had been painted on. I finally got the whole story out of him. It seems that another boy had referred to me as 'that old witch with a broomstick'. Gary, being a Leo, and a typical one at that, had sprung, obviously forwards, to my defence. His efforts seemed to be effective as there were no more black eyes or, as far as I knew, insults.

Once Gary asked me to read his hot chocolate cup at bedtime. I obliged. 'Gary,' I had to say, 'do be careful of the roads tomorrow—I mean specially careful.'

'Right, Mum,' he said, and went to sleep.

When I got home the next day, it was to a commotion. Apparently Gary had paid too much attention to a frog his cousin was carrying and too little to his road drill. He had stepped off the pavement and got knocked down. See Gary. See clairvoyance. Hates it!

Selina is a natural healer and people come to her with sick animals. I have never known her to be frightened of any animal, and they seem to sense this and will approach her of their own accord. There is a natural understanding between Selina and I. We often sit together in the evening and play a game of trying to guess each other's thoughts.

A client once gave me a gorgeous doll as a present for Selina. She loved it at first sight. I thought it looked just like an angel and suggested it should be called Angela.

'No,' said Selina firmly, 'she's Rose!'

I asked her why, but she did not seem to know. However, Rose it was.

Several weeks later, when the woman who had given the doll came for another consultation, I told her about Selina's insistence on the name Rose.

'That's funny,' she said. 'That's my middle name!'

Again, when we were on holiday in Devon in 1980, we went one evening to a country hotel for dinner. We were having drinks outside (it was the day that summer it didn't rain!) when a little black and white cat came out and joined us. Or rather it joined Selina.

'Aw, Mum,' she said, 'Isn't she gorgeous?'

'What do you think her name is?' I asked. I know too much about Selina's instinct to query her long-range sexing of a mere cat.

'Slippers,' she said. 'In fact, I *know* it's Slippers.'

When we went inside to have dinner, the cat and Selina having been parted from each other only with difficulty, the Head Waiter came up and talked to us, having worked in Glasgow and recognising our Glasgow accents!

'What's that cat's name?' I asked innocently, 'The little black and white one outside.'

'Oh,' he said, 'I think it's something to do with feet or shoes. . . . Slippers. Yes, that's it.'

I don't know how Selina knew. But I know why she knew.

Although, as I have said, my psychic powers became much stronger after Gary's birth, it still did not occur to me that I might be able to make more use of them.

When Gary was a baby I worked in a newsagents' shop for about two years, part time. I joined the Inland Revenue next and apart from a short time off to have Selina, my daughter, I was employed there for nine years.

I started as an ordinary clerkess. I couldn't help some of the things I said and people soon took notice of this small, chirpy, blonde who came out with extraordinary remarks which were nevertheless true. Then I got inveigled into giving lighthearted teacup readings in tea and lunch breaks.

'I see a close relation—your mother perhaps, going into a big building and signing her name,' I said to one girl. The next day she came in all bubbling. Unknown to her, her mother had been to the Employment Office . . . and had found herself a job!

For another I prophesied a visit from abroad by someone she had not seen or heard from for years. A few days later she had a letter from a long-lost cousin in South Africa, saying he was coming to Britain on a visit.

Some predictions were a bit bolder. 'You'll go on a journey this year and see the Empire State Building. . . .' I announced to one of our supervisors.

'No way,' she replied, with a laugh that was slightly bitter, 'A widow with two children, and on my salary!'

Several weeks later she won a soap-powder competition. The prize? I leave you to guess. . . .

Other predictions were more serious. One young girl, who sat behind me, passed me her cup one day. I looked at it, looked at her, and then I looked back at the cup. 'It's quite clear in here,' I said. 'You're going to have a daughter soon. Her name will begin with an S.'

'My Mum'll kill me if I do,' she said, and we burst out laughing at the thought. This girl wasn't married and showed no signs of being so.

However eleven months later she did have a baby, a girl, which she decided to call Susan. Her mother was not very pleased!

I remember very well the nice girl on the internal telephone exchange. I found myself having to warn her that the man she was going with was married. And I knew she had been seeing him for years. Clearly she did not do her detective work very well, or did not want to. She eventually married him, only later to discover that he had a wife already.

Soon my lunch hours ceased to be my own. I had begun to use other methods of prediction—Tarot and playing cards, and reading palms.

After nine years in the Inland Revenue, I developed a slipped disc. I was completely immobilised for three months. With the help of several doctors as well as an osteopath, my own healing ability and sheer willpower, I was eventually up and about again. I had been off work for almost a year. The children were now at school and I was driving myself mad just sitting at home during the day. I occupied myself by writing letters for publication in newspapers and magazines but I was looking forward to going back to work just to be *with* people when I was told firmly by my doctors that, what with diabetes and a weak back, a full-time job with all the travelling that would be involved would be too strenuous on top of being a housewife.

Never has anyone thought more fondly or wistfully about the Inland Revenue! I considered floristry again, but the shock of the experience at the time of the Cheapside Street fire was still with me. I felt I wanted to do something that would be of some definite help and use to people, but I did not have the right experience or qualifications for any job which had the necessary elements.

I considered all kinds of things and discarded each one in turn: the perfect solution took quite a long time to present itself.

Chapter 4
MAKING A NAME FOR MYSELF

AFTER some months of careful thought about what I could do to keep busy, be of use and, ideally, earn some money at the same time, I came up with the idea of being a fortune-teller . . . a professional fortune-teller! Once the idea was there, it was so obvious and simple a solution that I laughed at myself for not having arrived at it sooner.

The main reason that I took so long to think of it might have been that it was actually a very new idea. There had never been, in living memory, a professional clairvoyant in Scotland. Fortune-telling just hadn't existed as a job option! And after I had done it I was not surprised that no one else had tried . . . or perhaps they had tried and had given up. Given in when faced with the intricacies of modern life or with the realisation that the last trial for witchcraft in Britain was in Scotland, and that it *was* within living memory! However, once I have decided on something I am not easily deterred, and the family was right behind me. I guess they thought that they might get some fun out of it too, and I suppose they were right.

I wasn't quite sure how to set about becoming a professional clairvoyant, but the Glasgow Barras seemed a good place to start. The Glasgow Barras (or Barrows) is a large market area, colourful in every sense of the word, where almost anything can be bought and sold. It fairly overflows with people at the weekend. Perhaps I could set up a stall there?

So. . . . I went along and asked around. Could I have a place from which to operate? No, that sort of thing had

The Barras.

never been heard of before, so it couldn't be done. I went to the local police station. Could I have a caravan and park it in the street? No, I couldn't have a caravan and park it in the street. What *could* I do then? Ah, I could have a caravan and park it on a piece of private land. Eventually, after a lot of bother, I got my piece of land in the Barras. A prime spot, right next to the man who sold curtains by the mile!

So, I went out and bought a caravan ... for £80. George and I, with the two kids in the back of the car, towed it to the Barras every Saturday and Sunday. The caravan was blue and white, had four wheels ... and left a lot to be desired, for example the skylight, which had been blown off in a gale. George produced an old galvanised-iron dustbin lid, which he assured us was the answer. One day when we left for the market the sun was shining and the motorists were out in force. As they passed, cars hooted at us and their occupants gestured. Suddenly there was an almighty bang. We stopped dead and the dustbin lid, severely dented, flew by at terrifying speed and landed on the road with a resounding crash.

On another occasion George became convinced that the brake on one of the wheels was jamming. He finally got round to checking it and jacked up the caravan. The wheel fell off. Only the sheer weight of the caravan itself had kept it on the axle.

The Glasgow Barras is, to me, where the real people of the city congregate. The traders there buy and sell anything you can think of, and a few things you probably can't! Anyone who wants to learn how to sell should start there. Once my caravan was set up, I got an enormous amount of warm and generous help from the barrowmen (and women) round about.

The first weekend was quiet. I think I had three clients. The next weekend I had about ten, and from then on trade positively boomed. People came to see me in bus loads, from Edinburgh, Aberdeen and Dundee. One woman was on holiday from San Francisco. I told her that when she got home she would meet a man and that soon after she'd be wearing a new diamond ring. 'If ah ever get *that*, honey,' she said, 'ah'll invite you tuh the wedding.' I duly got an invitation. . . .

However success can ruin a small business. I could cope with only so many people in a day and some had to be turned away from the caravan. Clearly it was time for a move. I took a chance and rented an office at 16 Fitzroy Place in Glasgow, which I'd seen advertised in the evening paper. So far so good.

One night before moving into the office, I was having dinner with some friends. In the course of the evening the conversation turned to my new profession and it was suggested that I ought to have a professional name. One of those there, Alex Cameron of the *Daily Record*, suggested 'Darlinda'. I thought the name had a nice ring to it and asked how he had thought of it. 'It's my wee dog's name,' he replied! Nevertheless, I decided that I liked it and that, from then on, Darlinda I would be. Some years later I was doing a broadcast with the late Clark Tait of STV who asked how the name had come about. When I told him that it was Alex Cameron's dog's name, he quipped, 'thank goodness his dog wasn't called Spot' (or worse, come to think of it!).

There was a slight delay in my business starting up afresh in its rather smarter premises. The office had no phone, so I had to twiddle my thumbs until one could be installed. One day during this time I took the children to a riding school. While I waited for them I watched a photographer chatting up the models whose pictures he was taking. I went up to him.

'You must be a Gemini,' I said. It was a bit of a cheek but I simply had to do it.

'How did you know?' was all he said, hardly taking his eyes off his work (or his models!).

'I've been watching you for half-an-hour.'

'Yes, but how did you *know*?' he repeated, now a little interested in spite of himself.

So, in a rush, I explained that I had rented an office in Glasgow and that I was going to set up as Scotland's first professional clairvoyant—I'd checked up and no one had ever registered their name as one. He immediately asked if his newspaper could have the story, and not unnaturally I agreed (I would have given my story to *anyone* at that juncture).

I rang him up the day the phone was installed and sure enough, his newspaper, the *Sunday Mail*, sent up a reporter on my official 'opening day'. However that was nearly the *only* day I *was* open. . . .

'Are you sure you've got permission to operate as a clairvoyant?' was the reporter's opening gambit.

'Well . . . er,' I replied, 'when I was at the Barras they said that as long as I was off the street and on a piece of private land that was all right. And this is a piece of private land, isn't it?'

'I think you'd better check,' she said, and then went on with the interview.

So later I rang the police. I was passed from one department to another. No one wanted to know. I guess they thought I was mad. Finally I found someone who did want to know, and then I wished he didn't.

'Can't be done,' he said. 'And close the office within twenty-four hours if you don't want a warrant taken out.'

So I rang a lawyer. He didn't know anything relevant but he promised to look through his books. By three o'clock he had come up with an 1825 Vagrancy and Fraudulent Mediums Act which said that I could not use cheesecloth or a crystal ball. Otherwise, as long as I was not causing a public nuisance or actually doing anyone any harm, he reckoned I was in the clear. So I put my crystal ball away in a cupboard and went out and bought a glass paper-weight to take its place. Then I rang the police again to tell them the news.

My 'friend' sounded harassed. All he could say was, 'Well, for goodness' sake try to keep out of the news.' The police have not bothered me since and the publicity has not stopped flowing either.

My interview with Alison Goodall from the *Sunday Mail* resulted in a big splash in the paper the following Sunday. Within ten days of opening at Fitzroy Place, every appointment was filled and I had to employ a secretary to cope with the workload.

During the time I had the office at Fitzroy Place several strange things happened. For example, before Christmas one year we decided to hold an office party and invited some interesting people along to join us in

Mary Donachie, a runner up in the Miss Scotland contest, was a regular client at Fitzroy Place.

our celebrations of the Festive Season. Two of the guests were journalists from the *Sunday Mail*—Alex Scotland and the late John Sullivan—who dropped in for a drink after they had been out working on a story. The taxi driver who had brought them to the office joined us (to have a glass of Coke, of course). As the actual office was overflowing with guests, this small group joined Jimmy Robertson, the man who had the office next door, to stand out in the spacious entrance hall.

Given the occupation of their hostess it's not perhaps surprising that their conversation eventually came around to the subject of ghosts and spirits. The taxi driver expressed his severe scepticism, certain that such things were all in the imagination and a load of non-sense. All of a sudden a fire-door which was heavy and difficult to move, blew open, *outwards*, and a gust of freezing wind came swirling around the hall. It blew a poster bearing the cheery seasonal greeting 'Merry

Christmas' from the wall on which it had been firmly stuck. The gust departed swiftly. The poster fluttered to the floor and the door was once again shut tight. The taxi driver, scared out of his wits, departed swiftly too!

At the same office there was a small kitchen where we could prepare lunch. In the kitchen were six old-fashioned, well-rounded hooks where we hung our mugs. Within the space of three days all the mugs had to be replaced three times as they jumped off the hooks to smash on the hard floor beneath. Jimmy next door, a very sensible, clear-thinking chap, witnessed this and had no explanation for it. The hooks were deeply curved and no one could understand how on earth the mugs could just keep falling off on their own accord. It was an expensive week!

After eight years at Fitzroy Place, I moved to an office in Waterloo Street and from there, in 1983, to 8 Royal Crescent. There were some strange goings-on in Royal Crescent too.

One winter, on a Saturday between Christmas and New Year, a radio station in Dundee phoned to ask if I would talk to them about my predictions for the new year. When I agreed an outside broadcast team set off and a friend and I went in to open up the office for them. The phone rang and it was the team to say that they had broken down and would be an hour or so late. Some time later, as we waited in the second-floor office, we heard heavy footsteps coming up the stairs and we went out to meet our guests. There was no-one to be seen. We agreed that we must both have been hearing things but then it happened a second time and again our visitors were invisible. When the outside broadcast team did at last arrive they had great difficulty getting their equipment to record. Eventually they succeeded. Then, when they got back to Dundee they found that their tape was blank. In fact my predictions had been quite accurate but unfortunately no-one heard them!

One day a solicitor friend, Trevor Davis, dropped in to Royal Crescent for a coffee and to show me a ring. He asked me to hold it in my hand and tell him what I thought about it. I got a strong feeling of an old Jewish lady who had passed over. She was telling me she had eventually found her daughter Esmie, who had died tragically young. My friend was amazed as these details were perfectly accurate. The lady to whom the ring had belonged had died three months before, at the age of ninety-two. She and her husband had mourned all their lives since their daughter's early death.

Later that afternoon, alone in the office, I had a vision of two people in the room—a man and a woman—dressed in clothes of the 1930's or 40's. The man put his hands over my eyes. I got quite a fright but the lady assured me that the gentleman knew what he was doing and that my eyes would be okay. I had been having problems with my eyes at that time and was undergoing laser treatment. I told several people about this strange visitation and wondered what it was all about. Sometime later I found out from Ena, the secretary who had been employed in the office below mine for about twenty-five years, that before the building had been converted into offices in the 1950's it had been a dwelling house. The family who lived there were called Primrose. The husband and wife were both ophthalmologists who had practised in the Eye Infirmary which was situated near-by. The Primroses subsequently came back to visit me quite a few times.

The walls of my Royal Crescent office were decorated with photographs of many of the famous people I had met over the years since going in to the clairvoyance 'business'. One afternoon the photograph of Kenneth Williams, a charming man, came adrift and floated to the floor. Someone picked it up and placed it on the desk and minutes later we heard on the news that he had just died. Perhaps some of these strange goings-on were no more than unlikely coincidences. Perhaps there's more to it than that. These kinds of things seem to happen to me quite a lot!

Over the years my reputation grew by means of recommendation, and a steady stream of publicity ensured that the name 'Darlinda' became more and more widely known.

It wasn't long after opening at Fitzroy Place that someone at the BBC heard of me and my little 'business'. As a result, Bill Aitkenhead from *Good Morning Scotland* came down to interview me. I did a reading for him and, after telling him quite a lot about himself, he encouraged me to tell him quite a lot about myself—he's a very good interviewer! He was impressed by his reading, so much so that dozens of people from the BBC were phoning for appointments that same day.

Soon I was invited to appear on television. My first appearance on TV was in Aberdeen. The whole family set off on what was a full day's journey. At the studio I was introduced to a very polite man with a kindly face who spoke as though he had marbles in his mouth. I didn't catch his name, terrible nerves had my mind short-circuiting at the time! I did manage to grasp that he was one of the other guests on the chat show on which I was to appear. I was asked to read his hand—I suppose to give us something to talk about on the programme. I saw a wall tumbling, and warned him to be careful. There was someone he had loved but never married. I could see her name, and told him. It was obvious to me that he was a gentle soul because at this I could feel tears welling up into his eyes. I had been quite right. He had loved a girl who had died. It was not until a little time after I finished that I realised who he was—Lord Aberdeen.

What with Lord Aberdeen and his accent, and an Aberdeen fisherman and his dialect, I cannot say that I understood much of the chat during the show! I must have been all right, however, because I have been asked back many times since. (Oh, and the wall? Yes, one on Lord A's estate fell down a few days later. . . .)

Over the next few years I made many appearances on local TV and radio shows and featured frequently in the Scottish press. I began to feel that I was in danger of losing sight of reality. So I joined the Talbot Centre, a voluntary organisation in Glasgow which looks after down-and-outs. There's reality for you. I worked there every Wednesday night for two years. It could often be depressing to be with these people, whose lives seemed to have been ruined by weakness or misfortune. However there was a lot of hope there, and even some lovely moments. One day, Mother's Day, I was called over to a group of men (they were not over-clean to say the least of it). One of them held a posy of daffodils, bound firmly with insulating tape. He handed it to me. 'Happy Mother's Day Rita,' they chorused. It was a very tender moment and I must admit I shed a tear or two.

The posy was beautiful and when I got home I showed it proudly to the family. I took off the insulating tape. The posy disintegrated: all the stems were different lengths! My beautiful souls had stolen them from various parks in Glasgow! But they had gone to a lot of trouble and with all their problems they still had a thought to spare for me. I received other presents too while I was there. One evening a lovely but thoroughly grubby old man lay on the floor reverently holding a peppermint sweet. 'There ye are,' he said, and handed it up to me. I was as happy to accept it as he obviously was to give it . . . though I could never bring myself to eat it!

For several years all the publicity about Darlinda was in Scotland. At last the day came when I got a call from

London. Would I go down in two months' time for an audition for *Star Signs* on BBC 2. Would I? I'd never heard of *Star Signs* (there's always so much else going on that I haven't got much time to watch TV) but I had heard of BBC 2. So for the next six weeks I went regularly to an elocution teacher to improve my accent and make it more suitable for the show.

Once again the family upped sticks and trekked, but this time it was south. They can't get me all the way down here and then not use me on the programme, I had thought. Not a bit of it! When I arrived in the reception room, it was packed with London clairvoyants and teachers and practitioners of astrology, all milling around and waiting to be called. I felt very out of place. I couldn't even talk about the programme, as I'd never seen it.

At last, when my stomach was completely knotted up with fright, my call came. The room into which I was led did nothing to dispel my alarm. . . .

There was just a green baize table with a microphone growing out of the middle and two chairs. The top part of one wall was glass and behind it sat an imposing array of producers and the like. They could look down on me and hear me, but I could not hear them. It was like being in a fish tank!

A girl was brought in. She seemed a bit nervous. She sat down beside me.

'Now!' A disembodied voice crackled through the silence. I jumped and looked round for its owner. It clearly belonged to a producer-type behind the glass. 'I want you to read Miss Thompson's hand and say what you see. Take your time.'

I looked. I concentrated. Then all the cares and anxiety and even the row of people in the gallery above receded. I spoke in the vague direction of the microphone, in the poshest voice I could manage.

'Cut!' It was that uppity voice again, and I'd barely started. 'You've got a lovely Glasgow accent, my love, I know. Can we please have it?' All that money on elocution lessons, I thought. . . .

The girl was obviously acting under orders and sat silent throughout the reading of her hand. It was also as though her mind was deliberately blank. However this was not so much of a problem, as the lines and the signs were pretty clear. The main thing about her was that I saw she had just got engaged but her parents did not approve.

I finished. The girl went out, and I sat on, letting my mind and body relax as I try to do after every reading. When the voice broke into the silence again, it had an apologetic air about it.

'I'm sorry. Would you mind doing someone else's hand?'

Bring on the lions, I thought! To tell the truth I was beginning to enjoy myself.

My next 'client' turned out to be a woman who had been up in the gallery. I guessed she was an assistant producer or something. There was a lot to say from her hand and I could feel that she was not trying to hold anything back. To begin with I told her that she'd just found a ring which had been lost for years. She raised her eyes to look at me and nodded. She was having trouble with an elderly relative and something was wrong with her car. At this point she looked to the faces in the gallery and grinned. Her love life looked particularly fascinating and I was really warming to my task when a 'thumbs up' sign from her brought in the voice to close the proceedings.

The standard 'Don't call us, we'll call you' response was a real let-down after that, but they did tell me before we left the studios that the reason for sending in the second person was that the first reading had been more accurate than they had believed possible by normal methods.

The call came just two days later. I was to go down and appear on the programme. This is the big time, I thought. So apparently did most of my friends and acquaintances in Glasgow, who bombarded me with offers of clothes to ensure I was adequately dressed for the occasion. I turned them all down, including the mink coat and the fox fur jacket!

As the day drew closer, I began to have misgivings. I was going to appear on national TV not as myself, nor even in the role of counsellor that so many of my clients expect me to play, but rather as a participant in a parlour game. From a pair of hands thrust through a screen I would be required to tell to whom they belonged. The audience in the studio would be able to see both me and the person on the other side of the screen, and could, and would, react for all they were worth. It wasn't that I lacked confidence in my ability to do it—but it just didn't seem like *me*, especially when it came, as it certainly would come, to putting on an act for the cameras and the audience. But, as I consoled myself, the path to fame and fortune is never smooth or even rational.

The first thing that happened when we arrived on the day was that George was taken away and locked in a waiting room in the basement so that he could not find out who were the subjects on the programme. I was taken to another room for coffee and sandwiches. There followed a trial run in the studio, with technicians taking the parts of the two unknown personalities I would be required to identify from their hands.

Then the dressing, and the make-up and chronic jitters. It was all a far cry from the chat shows and the performances I had given before. I told myself that I wasn't trying to prove anything—just to do well enough to satisfy my family and all those lovely people in

Glasgow who had shown their interest (or concern) by bombarding the BBC with flowers and cards (over eighty of them) addressed to me, much to the dismay of the staff who had to cope with them.

Only bits of the show itself remain in my mind. The first pair of hands belonged to a male. I took them in mine and looked for clues. Artistic certainly. Actor probably. Most likely a funny man because the audience was soon in stitches over whatever it was he was doing on the other side of the screen. It was really more like *Twenty Questions* as I worked towards the solution. Then he started wiggling his fingers. 'You're someone who likes to carry on,' I said. Roar from the audience! I had it. Kenneth Williams.

The other guest was Susan George. In one way she defeated me, because I could not get her name; in another I was even more successful with her than I had been with Kenneth Williams for I predicted that she would make a good girlfriend for Prince Charles. Much later on their names *were* linked.

The evening ended, or one could say began, with a party in the BBC Hospitality Room. Susan George and Kenneth Williams were warm and hilarious. The hosts of the show, Frederick Davies and Michael Aspel, were particularly friendly and professional, the latter in spite of being a Capricorn! Then later the whole Glasgow contingent (there were five of us) went on to Frederick Davies' house for another party, clutching a bottle of gin we had originally bought for drinking in our hotel rooms—the off-licences were closed and Glaswegians never go to anyone's house without taking a contribution. We were expecting to be part of a crowd of several hundred, judging from the number of cards Frederick had been handing out in the BBC. But no! It turned out to be just us, our host, and three others. However we made enough noise, in our decorous Scottish way, to make up for that.

The programme had been recorded on the Thursday. We got back home on Friday night just in time to see it broadcast. I hid behind a cushion. Everyone was very kind about it. I was just pleased it was over and I could get back to my normal work. I was also suffering from acute nervous exhaustion and had to spend the weekend in bed.

On Monday morning, somewhat recovered, I went into the office and announced to my secretary, 'That's that. Back to work. Thank goodness. But at least I know now what it could be like to be a star.' At twelve o'clock the phone rang.

'BBC,' said my secretary, with just a hint of a smirk. The message was short and to the point. The show had been such a success that I was wanted on the second programme as well. Could I go down on Wednesday to be ready to record the following day? Oh no, not again, I thought. . . .

I had not known what to expect the first time. The second time I did know, and was four times as nervous. I even had to consult my doctor before I went down about a pulse that had started up in my throat. He confirmed that it was just nerves and said it would disappear the moment the show started. It did (auto-suggestion, perhaps?), and I've never had it since.

The personalities on the second show were Joanna Lumley and Peter Cook. I was not too good on the actual names (I thought Joanna was Una Stubbs) but their character analyses seemed to be pretty accurate.

The aftermath was very satisfying as several newspapers now took up my story and the *Sunday Mail*, which had given me my first break seven years before, invited me to be their resident astrologer.

TV appearances appear to breed more TV appearances. I was recruited for the STV Hogmanay show to celebrate the opening of 1980. Nothing much to it. .... I was just required, in front of an audience of millions and a star-studded cast, to announce my predictions for the year. I had done it for a *Sunday Mail* article the previous year (and had a 'good' year too in that seventeen of my twenty-four predictions—including the fall of the Shah—came true) and, two weeks before, they had printed what I had to say about 1980. But doing it on TV was very different.

Fortunately, I had already had a good break in that among my *Sunday Mail* predictions for 1979 had been the unlikely one of an earthquake in Scotland. Scotland had experienced its earthquake just six days before, on Boxing Day 1979, and the programme presenter duly made a great deal of the fact. Well, the Hogmanay programme turned out to be great fun. When the time came for my spot—to broadcast my predictions for 1980—I was feeling relaxed and confident, as you can imagine most of Glasgow is on Hogmanay—even those appearing on TV!

Over the years I have been fortunate to meet many very interesting people some of whose names and faces are familiar to all. Diana Dors was as lovely inside as she was outside. I first met her when she came for a consultation. She was doing a programme in Glasgow and found herself with time to spare. Having heard some people in the TV studios discussing me, she made an appointment. She was stunned by the accuracy of her first reading. After a number of consultations we got to know each other well and eventually became close friends.

She often came to Glasgow to visit me and I visited her at her home in Sunningdale, Berkshire. I would do a reading for her and explain what was happening to her from her natal astrological chart, then we would sit and chat for hours. Eventually I felt that I knew her as well as she knew herself.

She was a very clever and astute lady with a wonderful sense of humour who could laugh at life and at herself. She had a wonderful radiance and presence. She phoned me in the February before she died and hoped to come to Glasgow later that month. She never managed the journey.

One day about two months after her death I was rather surprised when my secretary announced that Diana's husband, Alan Lake, was on the phone. Apparently Diana had told him just before she died that she would contact him through me, using me as a medium. He was disappointed when I told him she hadn't been in touch. In August that year, one afternoon when I was writing my column for the *Sunday Mail*, I was suddenly distracted and, when I looked up, Diana was standing in the middle of the room wearing a cerise-coloured dress. She told me that it had taken quite a time to get over to the other side and that it had been a very rough passage but now that she had arrived she was happy and content. She had met lots of her old pals and was delighted they were there with her. She was worried about her sons, Gary and Jason. She then asked me to ask Alan not to go through with what he was thinking about as there was plenty of time and she would always be there waiting for him. She was sorry his back pain had recurred and she would continue to massage it for him. She now realised how much they loved one another.

I phoned Alan only to find that he had gone away for the weekend. I left for Spain the next day for a two-week holiday.

On returning I learned that Alan had telephoned my home and my office several times and had even tried to contact me in Spain. I phoned him immediately. I heard how he was going through hell and found it impossible to live without Diana. I told him what Diana had said to me a fortnight before and asked him to be strong and courageous for the sake of his sons. I was more than shattered a few weeks later when I heard on the 5 p.m. news on *Radio Clyde* that Alan had taken his own life.

Since gaining a reputation I have been invited to work abroad on a number of occasions. In 1980 I worked in Toronto for three weeks, doing consultations and several TV and radio shows. I liked the Canadian people. Most of those I met had emigrated from places like Govan, Lanark or Renfrew so I felt quite at home! I still get many invitations to go back.

I have worked in Marbella a lot and have enjoyed meeting a great many of the famous and colourful personalities who live there. Their lives are fascinating, particularly when I am often able to tell them the things they are trying to keep secret. Some of the world's top businessmen (and a few 'top' crooks) have consulted me there.

I was once invited to a party on a large yacht where a gold Rolex seemed to be the badge of the club and the women seemed to have stepped straight out of *Dynasty*. The guests were all (or all but one!) extremely rich and had made their fortunes in an interesting variety of ways! I spoke to one man who had been on the run from the police in the UK for fifteen years but was still running businesses in several different countries. This man burst out crying when I mentioned the name of his little Yorkshire Terrier that had died.

We have made a lot of friends on the 'Costa del Crime', none of them criminals I hasten to add! The whole area is particularly beautiful and I always feel on a psychic high when I am there.

But I really love Glasgow. To me it's the most beautiful city in the world with the warmest and friendliest people! I do quite a few public appearances now and I feel I have become part of the character of Glasgow. I'm very proud of that, and my Glasgow accent.

Very recently we went along to a charity dinner. The cabaret star was Brenda Cochrane, who had recently won *Opportunity Knocks*. Before her act, Paul Cooney of *Radio Clyde*, the compere, announced to the audience that I had predicted Brenda's win ages before (but then that would have been easy for anyone to predict— she has a super voice and is great entertainment). I've got used to being a celebrity at such occasions but it still sometimes takes me by surprise when people come up to me in airports, restaurants and the like and thrust their palms in my direction for an instant reading (I don't know why it should surprise me as it happens quite often!) For example, one day in a restaurant I noticed that a woman was looking at me very oddly. Suddenly she gobbled down her food, dived towards me and pushed a ring into my hand. The ring had apparently been given to her many years before by her husband and she was wondering, if I held it, whether I could tell from the vibrations where he had run off to and with whom!

My local supermarket is a perpetual source of such confrontations. I have learned to spot people who look as though they might demand an instant interview at the cheese counter, and keep clear of them. (Oh well, no cheese this week!). An equally common reaction seems to be amazement that I am buying washing powder rather than 'eye of newt', and that I go round the shelves with a trolley instead of on a broomstick!

Chapter 5
THE BLACK, BLACK CLOUD
AND THE SILVER LINING

ALTHOUGH I have been a diabetic for more than thirty years, I have enjoyed good health and have never thought of the diabetes as an illness. I coped with 'it' and 'it' coped with me and I have led a very full, busy, happy life. I had heard and read about the complications related to diabetes but, like most bad things in life, I felt they couldn't happen to me. Then, in 1985, my health began to deteriorate week by week. Where had all my energy gone? Why was life becoming such a trial? My generally happy, bubbly nature was less and less evident. At the back of my mind was the terrible thought of renal failure and although my brother, who was also diabetic, had died from this illness, I still tried to put it out of my mind. Eventually I went along to visit Dr. Ken Patterson at the Southern General Hospital in Glasgow who had the gruesome task of telling me I was indeed suffering from renal failure and I would soon have to go on to dialysis. That particular day the world seemed to stop. Rita just couldn't cope. The days after that got greyer as they dawned.

My partner, Rajan, who is a doctor, became my strength. He helped to give me the courage that was lacking but even then, at times, I felt that I could never face what was in front of me. I felt I was the weakest person in the world: how could everyone else be so brave?

I went along to the Renal Unit at Glasgow's Western Infirmary for the first time, and I was lucky enough to see one of the marvellous consultants, Dr. Brian Junor, who clearly explained the two methods of dialysis. Prior to going to the clinic I had made up my mind that I wanted to be put on a kidney machine (haemodialysis) twice a week for four hours and this would get it over with. The alternative was to have fluid permanently sloshing around in my abdomen, changed every four hours through a catheter (tube) which would be inserted into my abdomen at my waist. This method is called peritoneal dialysis and was definitely not for me. I wasn't going to walk around with a catheter hanging out of me—the thought was just awful.

Well, fifteen minutes with Dr. Junor changed my mind. I don't know if it was a case of gentle persuasion or just the charming authority of his voice but I left the clinic knowing that changing bags of fluid was eventually going to become part of my everyday routine whether I liked it or not, and probably for quite some time.

I just about survived for a year feeling wretched, being sick, waiting for the poisons in my body (urea and creatinine) to get to a high enough level and then I would start on dialysis. One Saturday morning I just couldn't stop being sick and felt really miserable. We phoned the Western Infirmary and spoke to the more senior consultant, Dr. Briggs, and he made the immediate decision that the time had come for the dreaded dialysis. I was actually almost relieved to hear him confirm this as I was feeling just so unwell.

I was admitted to Level Seven at the Western on a Monday morning and on Tuesday had the operation to have the catheter inserted. On the following Monday I attended the Renal Unit to start on my treatment. When I saw all the tubes and sterile equipment I thought that I would never be able to master the technique of changing the fluid. However, with careful and understanding tuition from the nursing staff I was soon quite confident and had begun to adjust to my new way of life. Two days later I was feeling well enough to drive myself to the hospital and had a smile back on my face again. I really was beginning to feel much better. I had mastered the whole technique by the Thursday and was able to do it on my own, at home, on the Friday.

During my year of dialysis, the exchanges took place in many strange places. As I had to perform the procedure four-hourly, and it took approximately one hour to do, the bags of sterile fluid and all the equipment went with me in my car wherever I went. Several times I had to do the exchange in my car at the side of a road, and hotel rooms witnessed the changing of the bags too. At social functions, I wore maternity evening wear as peritoneal dialysis makes you look several months pregnant! At first, people would wonder why I would disappear for an hour without explanation and would be surprised when I told them I was doing my exchange. They soon got used to it, however, and would simply nod and smile as I slipped away and slipped back again an hour or so later. Life doesn't just stop because of kidney failure and I made up my mind that it wasn't going to get me down—it was going to live with me as my diabetes had done. My family and friends were wonderful—they were extremely supportive and gave me the encouragement that I needed. Friends would volunteer all sorts of services but I was so determined not to be an invalid that I wouldn't accept. At least I always accepted company and I was never on my own for long. One day I had fourteen unexpected visitors at the same time, three of them were called Anne and two called Anna. You can imagine the confusion and hilarity in our house that afternoon! I always pretended to be so brave on the surface but sometimes I shed a few wee private tears. Rajan always knew when I was feeling like this and I know he often felt the same but he would never show it. Instead he would shout some nice abuse at me—tell me to stop feeling sorry for myself—so that I would be roused to argue, and then get on with things. He knew how to handle me. When I was on dialysis, some days I was so tired and weary that it was a big decision even to make myself a cup of tea but Gary and Selina were usually around to dance attendance!

There were some really awful times. I remember one particular morning I felt so dreadful that I headed for the clinic at the Western where I was greeted by Dr. Junor. I was so ill and disorientated, that all I could say to him was 'Dr. Junor, I think I'm falling to bits.' He smiled and, in his own charming, quiet way, assured me that I would stay in one piece— talk about Humpty Dumpty!

I still worked in my office at Royal Crescent during this period. The two flights of stairs to my office were steep so I would often have to take several rests, sitting on the stairs, on my way up. Parking my car was another problem; I often had to find a space that I could drive into as I hadn't the energy to manoeuvre into a space. The secretary working in the office downstairs would heat the bag of dialysis fluid on top of her radiator to make sure it was warm enough for me to use at lunch time.

Very few people in life get off altogether without having a bout of ill health either themselves or within their families. I think it gives people a great deal of extra understanding when it happens. Being so well known in Glasgow, I couldn't go anywhere without someone asking how the dialysis was going. I hope that I may have made people more aware of what happens when the kidneys fail.

Throughout my period of dialysis the thought of a kidney transplant was the magic, beautiful light at the end of the tunnel. It gave me a lifeline to hang on to and I certainly hung on with a tight grip.

Every day I expected the phone call. Even if I was

having a meal in a restaurant, hearing a phone ring, I would think 'a kidney'. The thought of a transplant was never far from my mind. Many people said, 'Being psychic, do you not know yourself whether and when a kidney transplant might be offered to you?' I can see things for other people but it's different for myself. However, according to the transits in my astrological chart I was fairly sure it had to take place sometime between April and June so when that time came I packed my bag—packed with positive thought, I may add—and put it in the boot of my car.

On the morning of May 18th, I attended the memorial service in Milngavie for my dear friend Sir Hugh Fraser. I had all sorts of strange feelings during that day and in the evening couldn't settle to anything constructive. I had a bath and a shower, washed my hair, did my nails, wrote some letters, phoned some friends and told them I was feeling rather odd (one of them remarked that that was not unusual!)

My sister Margaret Mary suggested that perhaps the next day would be my lucky day, that I would be offered a kidney. The next day would be a Tuesday and she had always known that the transplant would take place on a Tuesday because of special prayers she had been saying. When I went to bed that Monday night I lit a candle at my bedside for comfort—I just knew something was going to happen. . .

I was woken by the phone ringing at 5.30 in the morning and heard a lovely voice saying 'Hello, this is Elaine from the Renal Unit at the Western. Do you know why I am phoning you?' I almost danced with excitement and hope. Elaine confirmed that they did indeed have a kidney for me and Rajan was left to organise things as Selina, my daughter, and I went wild with delight. I quickly phoned my sisters and two of my friends. I remember my sister Margaret Mary saying that it was just as though when Sir Hugh met God he said 'Rita's had enough of that dreaded dialysis, it's time you found a kidney for her!' Then I set out for the Western Infirmary with a feeling of total euphoria. The car journey was like taking a journey through heaven. The road from Carswellbank across Kennishead Road and then Pollokshields never looked like this before—everything was just so beautiful. Even the motorways looked magic. We noticed two magpies on the grass verge of the motorway—two for joy! The old buildings in Argyle Street looked like a sparkling city. I had to keep pinching myself to make sure it wasn't only a dream.

I was in the hospital within half an hour of the wonderful phone call. There I was met by Dr. Briggs who explained everything to me and hinted that the operation didn't carry a guarantee.

Mr Stuart McPherson, the surgeon with magic hands, came to see me to tell me that he would go ahead with the operation at 10 a.m. From 5.30 a.m. until 10 a.m. felt like only minutes. I remember everyone being so nice in the theatre. They seem to know just how a patient feels and are able to say just the right thing at exactly the right time. Three and a half hours later the kidney was transplanted and started to work instantly. Afterwards, I remember being pushed along a corridor and a nurse saying 'Look what's arrived for you already' and showing me a gorgeous bouquet of blue and pink flowers. These had been sent by a gentleman friend, George Proudfoot, a national newspaper distributor, who had heard of my operation over his car radio on the lunchtime news. This was the first sign of the enormous warmth and love that I was to be shown over the period of my convalescence.

The care one gets after a transplant is tremendous. The doctors, the sisters, the charge nurses and the nurses are absolutely wonderful. My every whim was satisfied and nothing appeared to be a bother. I know these angels must have their own problems but these were never evident. I saw nothing but smiling faces all the time. These people, on whom I was so dependent, became like a family with a bond of real love being formed.

When I realised I had five tubes going into my neck and two other tubes going elsewhere, there wasn't much to do but lie very still. In any case I *couldn't* do much else as I was feeling so weak and sore. Would I ever be strong again?

In the evening of that wonderful day I was delighted to see my visitors. They all just stood looking at me and my tubes and wires in dismay. I'm sure they looked worse than I did—it's a sight I will never forget—they couldn't even speak.

It's amazing what a difference a day makes. By day two, I could move my legs a little and my voice had come back. The next day I was sitting up on a chair (although getting there had been pure hell). I continued to recover steadily and by the eighth day was allowed home. Delighted to be home but still very weak I continued to improve until the following week. Then a little hiccup occurred with the kidney. There were some signs of rejection. I'm sure now that it only happened to make me realise that I shouldn't be complacent. Such a thing can occur at any time. Although I can live life to the full again I should appreciate every minute of it.

After the operation I received over forty baskets and bouquets of flowers and over 300 'get well' cards. People of many different religions were saying prayers for me. The man above listened to every one of them. I am convinced that all of these prayers, thoughts and good wishes made a real contribution to my speedy recovery. I am so grateful for them all.

I am also, of course, truly grateful for my kidney.

The only awful thing about a kidney transplant is that my happiness is matched, somewhere, by another family's grief. All transplant recipients are infinitely grateful to all those who carry kidney donor cards. I encourage all my family and friends to do so.

Once home, my mind was full of all the things I had to do in thanks for my new life. When I was on dialysis I decided I must raise some cash for Kidney Research. However, I had been so ill and tired during my dialysis that although mentally bright, I was a physical wreck and had been dragging my heels. I was angry with myself for having been so 'lazy'.

During the past three years, since my transplant, I have successfully raised and handed over £50,000 to Renal Research and already have £25,000 towards the next £50,000!

Handing over the first instalment to Dr. Briggs of the Western Infirmary. Helping me is my nephew, Paul Hayes, who raised £67 by doing a sponsored crawl when he was seven months old!

I thank God every morning for my kidney and thank him for the experts in the Renal Unit. It is a miracle that I am alive and I am determined not to waste a second of my wonderful new life. I treat each day as a new experience. I take time to stop and smell the roses and I try to meet at least one new person every day. I have never felt so healthy before. I walk my two huge German Shepherd dogs every morning for about two miles before starting my day's work. In fact I have to be reminded to take a rest at times! There certainly is life after transplantation. In fact, I have found life to be more precious and wonderful the second time around. They say that every cloud has a silver lining—in this case they're absolutely right.

Chapter 6
BUSINESS AS USUAL

A S YOU can imagine, most of my professional life is taken up with consulting.

I consult for one day each week in Glasgow where my appointments book is bulging. (However, much as I enjoy my work it is very tiring and I have other things that I like to do.) I also spend, on average, one day a month consulting elsewhere in the UK, usually London, and of course am further kept busy preparing my weekly horoscope column for the *Sunday Mail*.

When someone comes along to consult me the first thing I do to put the client at ease is try to befriend him or her and chat about anything that comes into my mind. Sometimes the chat is about the weather, sometimes about some local event, sometimes even about the clothes we are wearing. Anything at all that helps to relax the client and helps him to forget that I am going to become part of him for the next half hour and that I am going to look into his psyche and his forward thinking mind.

I ask him to clear his mind of all thoughts that have been concerning him over the day and ask him to select thirteen Tarot cards. Clients usually ask 'Why thirteen?' They are surprised when I tell them that it's my lucky number. The only time I dislike thirteen is when the thirteenth falls on a Friday. I used to be terrified to drive or do anything of importance on this day but now I'm glad to report that I'm not quite so paranoid. Anyway back to the Tarot cards: when the thirteen cards are selected, I place them down on the table in a shape which resembles a Christmas tree; I always hope that the client has selected happy and good cards but it doesn't always work out that way. Anyone can learn to read Tarot cards but the psychic powers of the reader are of great importance. It's just the same with astrology. Anyone can take a course in astrology and can spout facts about planets and transits as if her tongue is replaying messages from a text book but when it comes to interpretation she can be miles off the mark—success depends upon how psychically gifted the clairvoyant or astrologer is.

After I read the Tarot cards I use either ordinary playing cards or at the moment a pack of cards which I bought in France called The Belline Fortune Cards. I love these cards. I get all sorts of wonderful messages and meanings from them. In the same way as I use the Tarot, thirteen of these cards are selected and read.

I then read the palm. I always read the left palm although I have heard that the gypsies prefer to read the right. I ask the client to stretch their hands out in front of me and I touch the tips of their fingers from which I get all sorts of weird and wonderful feelings. Lots of people have natural healing powers and I sometimes get my batteries recharged while I'm looking into the future by touching their fingers. Our hands carry pictures of what is in store for us and also show our strengths and weaknesses. Lines on the hands are of course of utmost importance but when I look deeply into the palm of someone's hand I can often see pictures of what is going to happen in the future or of events that have happened in the past. Often people feel frightened because there is a break in their life line but they are wrong to think that this is an indication of a short life. My mother had a very definite break in her life line and she lived until she was eighty-four! After reading the client's palm, I then go on to read the crystal. I ask my client to place the crystal on her left hand and cover it with her right hand; while doing this she should make a wish. When I look into the crystal I can see if the wish will be granted or not. If it is going to be granted, little stars will come up into the crystal just like a little fountain, but if it's not going to be granted the crystal will remain clear. When I gaze into the crystal it's almost as though I'm looking at a miniature television set as all sorts of pictures and faces come up on it. Sometimes faces of the people on this earth or often people who have departed long ago.

The routine of a consultation is usually the same, from sheer habit. The 'props' I use are means towards an end; they do not on their own provide the answers. The 'crystal ball' is merely an aid to concentration. So, to a lesser extent, is someone's palm—the lines are starting points for what I can see lies behind and beyond them. With the cards, what matters is the way I find myself interpreting their messages more than just seeing the messages themselves.

Once I have completed these four different methods of divination I allow my client to ask three important questions, After each question I ask them to select seven Tarot cards and these seven cards give the answer to the question.

Although these are the methods I use for a consultation there are many, many more methods of looking into the future. Reading tea leaves is one of the easier methods. Autumn leaves broken up by crushing them between your hands then dropping them on a white surface is very much like reading tea leaves. If you are psychic enough it's possible to read anything you set your mind to.

I do not pretend that my psychic perception is, on its own, any more infallible than, say, astrology, which after all is accepted as a genuine science in many quarters. I would contend however that when I combine that psychic sensibility with astrological findings or with any of the other methods of prediction I use, the chances of accuracy are multiplied. Certainly, to judge also from the appointments book in my office, my rate of success is not such that could be achieved by mere guesswork or even intelligent observation. Be that as it may, there is a sense in which people come to me also for genuine assistance or reassurance over something which is causing them trouble or pain. This has less to do with 'telling the future' than with helping them to face the present.

Last week I received a letter from Lynda in Australia. I first got to know her about five years ago when she visited my office in Royal Crescent. Lynda had been brought up by foster parents who eventually adopted her, but she had always yearned to find her real parents. I told her during a consultation then that I felt her mother was living in Australia. Later she came back with a map and I was able to say where approximately Lynda would find her mother. At the same time, as I always say in a situation like this, I asked her if she didn't feel she should leave things as they were as not to do so might cause a lot of hurt. Anyway Lynda went off on her long journey and eventually found her real mother who was suffering from multiple sclerosis and was now in a wheelchair. Lynda is convinced she has done the right thing. I am not so sure, as I believe in the old saying, 'Let sleeping dogs lie'. Perhaps I would feel differently in her situation.

I am never completely sure that I am doing the right thing in cases like this. I have to be very careful what I say when someone comes along to consult me. I may see, for example, that a client's partner is seeing someone else. I have to be very ambiguous, be really gentle with my words when this happens. Usually the person who consults me actually knows and they are just wanting it confirmed.

Lots of other people come along who have found another partner and just want it confirmed that the person they have met has the same feelings as they have. I hate it when my Tarot cards and feelings say no—but I can't tell them lies. Other people get into terrible trouble with financial matters and live in the hope that they are going to win the pools. I always try to, and usually do, find a little bit of light at the end of the tunnel.

Sometimes I have to break bad news about something that has not yet happened. I may need to do this, especially if it means that my client will be better off for being prepared for it or being able to take action to lessen the blow when it comes. This calls for their having a strength of character the extent of which I need instinctively to assess before I say anything, as well as tact on my part in the telling. If I feel, as I several times have felt, that a woman's husband is in danger of having a heart attack, it is more important that she should, for instance, be warned that a serious illness is imminent in her family and (later on in the interview) that any pains in her husband's chest should not be dismissed as indigestion or office strain, than that he should die for lack of care. When, as also has happened, the husband is as a result in hospital for observation within hours, the decision and the anxiety on my part are justified.

I once warned a girl who came to my office to see a doctor as there could be problems with her blood. She phoned me a few weeks later to tell me that she had taken my advice and that the hospital to which the doctor had referred her had diagnosed leukaemia at its earliest (and most curable) stage.

Many clients simply can't see the wood for the trees. Talking to them unravels their minds so that before they leave they are much more settled and know what their next step and probably the outcome will be.

When the client leaves the room, I often feel utterly drained, physically as well as mentally, and sometimes have to run cold water over my hands and wrists to freeze and somehow dispel the sensations I have assumed from my client. This is especially the case where the sensations have been those of pain or fear or guilt.

Of course the office also attracts all sorts of weird and wonderful people. There was the seventy-year-old who claimed she was Marlene Dietrich and proceeded to sing several of her numbers to prove it.

There at first appeared nothing strange about the girl who came on another occasion. Then, during the reading I kept getting the name 'Aida'. I thought at first it must be Ada. But no, Aida persisted. I asked the girl about it.

'Oh, no,' she said, unsurprised. 'It's Aida all right. That's the Egyptian spirit that has been with me for months now.'

Aida was an Ethiopian princess about whom Verdi wrote his famous opera of the same name.

The girl went on to tell me at great length and in considerable depth how some time before she had got an urge to find out everything she could about ancient Egypt. She bought every book on the subject. She visited museums. She tried to come into contact with Egyptian artefacts of all kinds. She bought facsimiles of Egyptian jewellery and danced in front of the mirror wearing them. At this point she became convinced either that she was 'Aida' or that a spirit of that name was trying to get into her earthly body. As always, I tried to behave as though I met Egyptian spirits regularly, but I did advise her to fight against it, as indeed I sensed she had the ability to do. However, if you ever should see a tall dark girl walking down the street in Egyptian garb, her arms arranged in the shape of a Z, you will know she is still fighting. . .

Such visitors to the office are not frightening. Some have been, however. There was the man who was given

82

an early appointment as a result of a continuous bombardment of pleas by a friend from a local radio station. This client turned out to be obsessed with blood, knives and tonsils. He offered to cut out my tonsils and invited me to visit his university laboratory to see the tonsils he *had* cut out, and, as an extra, to sleep with him overnight in a graveyard! Fortunately I was able to get rid of him without agreeing to any of his proposals!

About six years ago a top Glasgow businessman was on trial at the High Court on a fraud case. Before the trial he had come along to consult me and I told him the jury would find him not guilty. John Dowdall, the advocate, was working hard for him but the newspapers were appearing to point a guilty finger at him. During the case the gentleman kept saying to himself, 'Darlinda said I would be found not guilty'. The trial lasted for several days and I waited anxiously for the result, listening carefully to every news bulletin. When the final verdict came I was sent a case of champagne, phew!!! I don't always get such instant and gratifying feedback when my predictions are shown to be accurate!

From time to time my work takes me out of the country.

One January morning in 1980, for example, I came into the office and said, 'Don't take any appointments for September. I'm going abroad. On business.' I added for good measure.

My secretary opened the diary and made a note in it. 'Where?' she asked.

I thought, 'Where on earth *am* I going?'

'I don't know,' I answered rather lamely.

'Then how do you know you are going?'

'It just came to me,' I said.

In due course I had an invitation to make my first professional visit to Canada . . . in September. To anyone less psychic I suppose it would have come 'out of the blue'.

I then created an astrological chart for myself for the end of the year and discovered that I was due to travel abroad also in November and in January of the next year. So I did not make any appointments for those months either, thus avoiding any possibility of disappointing clients. Needless to say the chart was right— much nearer the time my agent in Canada rang me to ask if I could hold myself ready to repeat the trip at intervals of two months. And while I was in Canada I had no need to keep a diary of my appointments. George, at that time my husband and the resident family astrologer, had supplied me with an individual chart which told me in advance (and as it turned out, with one hundred per cent accuracy) exactly what I would be faced with each day.

One of the strangest and most frightening spells of my career as a clairvoyant was in 1981. In retrospect, it was almost like a chapter from a political thriller, and it was only when it was all over that I realised what a lucky escape I had had.

While on a working visit to London in June 1981, I was introduced by the singer Callum Kennedy's daughter, Fiona, to the then art director of the glossy women's magazine *Cosmopolitan*. She was so impressed with her reading that she mentioned my name at a jet-setters' cocktail party she happened to be at some days later.

At this function was rich Maltese businessman called Dione—who was a member of the opposition party back in Malta, a very troubled country at that time. Malta was in the throes of political turmoil. The Prime Minister, Dom Mintoff, was pushing his country into some unsavoury alliances with the likes of Colonel Gadaffi of Libya, arms dealers in Iran and the Soviet government.

Dione and his fellow Nationalists were outraged at the destructive path which they saw Mintoff carving out for their country.

To their eyes, Mintoff was putting Malta out on a

limb and cutting them off from Western allies such as Britain and Italy.

Mintoff had already kicked the Royal Navy out of the strategically vital capital of Valletta, and the Nationalist party officials—many of whom were businessmen like Dione—were terrified that their important trade links with Britain and other Western countries might be jeopardised. Probably most agonising for the Maltese people, Mintoff was intent on seizing the considerable assets of the Catholic Church on the island. And Malta, with its historic links with St. Paul and the origins of the Christian faith, was almost one hundred percent Catholic.

This man Dione—who was used to getting his own way in everything—asked to have a consultation with me.

I agreed to see him in London a few days after the party and he subsequently travelled to see me in Glasgow on a number of occasions. Over a period of six months I told him a number of things which inevitably came true regarding investments and business interests.

I warned him to be wary of an Arab gentleman with whom he was doing business. He was about to sign a deal with him and I told him on *no account* should he enter into any pact with him. I later found out that one of Dione's friends had gone ahead with the deal and had ended up losing thousands of pounds.

I also recounted details of his past—such as the death of his friend and facts about his private life which apparently no-one could have known.

Towards the end of 1981 he asked me a great favour. Would I come to Malta just after Christmas for a week? He said over and over again that he had many friends who desperately wanted to consult with me.

Well what could I say? I was on holiday and he told me it wouldn't interfere with my family Christmas and

New Year because I would leave on Boxing Day and come back before New Year's Eve.

Ridiculous as it may seem, I was totally oblivious to the fact that Malta had, just one week before I went there, been through one of its bitterest elections ever.

I have never been particularly interested in politics and, well, there's always so much going on at Christmas time that I must just have missed the news.

Dione's party, the Nationalists, had lost again to Mintoff and accusations were flying that Mintoff had rigged the election results. In fact, as it turned out, Mintoff's ruling Labour Party had got 4,000 votes less than the Nationalists but some artful reorganisation of electoral districts had given him a three seat majority!

It was a terrible wrench leaving my family and friends on Christmas night as I boarded an overnight bus, from a deserted Glasgow Buchanan Street bus station, to London. I had to take the bus on Christmas Day because there were no trains running and I had to catch a flight to Malta early on December 26.

There was a pathetic clutch of people on the bus. One woman sticks out in my mind. She had heard of the death of a close relative and taking the overnight bus on Christmas night was the only way she could travel to be near her family.

Frankly, it was a bad beginning and I didn't set out in a particularly positive frame of mind.

I arrived in a lukewarm Malta just before lunchtime on Boxing Day and was met by a reception committee comprising Dione and two small friendly men dressed in dark suits.

Only my host Dione could speak English but all three men were very welcoming and hospitable and treated me with the utmost respect—in fact their welcome was quite overwhelming. I felt like a conquering heroine.

They whisked me off in a sleek black car to a luxurious hotel by the sea where I was shown to a splendid suite which had a beautiful view looking onto the deep azure blue of the Mediterranean.

Very politely, they requested that I inform my non-English speaking 'bodyguard'—who was posted outside my room—if I wanted to go anywhere.

At this point I began to wonder what exactly I had got myself into.

Over the next few days the same thought was often to flash into my head as I was paraded around various meeting places on the island.

Everywhere we went it was obvious that Dione commanded much respect on Malta. I remember one incident particularly. It happened the day after Boxing Day when Dione and the two businessmen drove me off to a village high in the mountains. On the way there, in the darkness, strange lights flashed on and off to let my hosts know that all was well ahead.

When we reached our destination it was ten o'clock at night and the place was buzzing with excitement as though our arrival had been eagerly awaited by the village folk. They all seemed to have one thing in common—hatred of the Prime Minister, Dom Mintoff.

A man duly arrived who turned out to be Eddie Fenech Adami, leader of the Nationalist party—Mintoff's arch political rival.

His followers had raised money to buy him a Mercedes car and he was to be presented with it that night. The whole affair was shrouded in secrecy.

Why the secret venue? Why under cover of darkness? I knew that Mintoff's governing party would have been outraged at the goings-on. There was probably more subterfuge that evening but I was only given sketchy details of what was happening.

I know for sure that I felt completely caught up in the heady atmosphere created by the fervour these people had for their country and their political beliefs.

After the keys of the Mercedes were handed over to Adami there was a flurry of flash bulbs and I found myself being photographed right, left and centre. We all smiled happily for the cameras which, although I didn't realise it at the time, belonged to photographers from the unofficial newspaper of the Nationalist Party.

I had the feeling more than once during my time in Malta that Dione had created an image of me as a Joan of Arc figure—brought by him to his homeland to lead the people out of their misery. And I certainly glimpsed both sides of Malta when I was there. At that time it was very much a divided island of opulence on the one hand and poverty on the other.

Later that night we saw the two sides come together when we went to the village social club. It was packed with people who looked down-at-heel and miserable. They were poorly dressed and drinking the only thing they could afford—the local beer.

The minute we stepped in there was an immediate hush and a path cleared for Adami, Dione and his entourage, who steered themselves effortlessly towards the bar. Expectation hung in the air and it became clear we were held in awe by the crowds who had gathered especially for the occasion.

Dione ordered drinks for our little group and I talked to the only other English speaker—a Maltese MP who was also a solicitor with a lot of business in London.

All round I could hear the unfamiliar and unsettling sound of people speaking in a foreign tongue as he explained to me a little about the muddled state of Maltese politics at that time, and how it was imperative that they kick Mintoff out to save the island from what they saw as his destructive influence.

The next day I was driven to the home of one of the men who had met me at the airport, to meet his wife and family. His mansion was breathtaking, extravagantly furnished and indicating enormous wealth.

His wife was small and rounded and seemed absolutely enthralled at meeting me as though she had been given a glowing account of what I was like. The Joan of Arc syndrome was at work again. She sat me down and fed me with a delicious meal on which she had obviously spent a lot of time and energy.

Every day followed a similar pattern. I was driven to see people who believed I was in possession of almost magical powers and had it in me to bring down the Mintoff government.

On the sixth day of my seven day stay the picture that had been taken of me with Adami appeared in his Nationalist party newspaper. Everywhere I went people seemed to know who I was and smiled happily as they waved a copy of the paper at me.

By this time I was beginning to wonder what my role was in Adami's political manoeuvring. Everything Dione and his friends did was in true cloak-and-dagger style. If they didn't want me to know what was happening they spoke in Maltese—and that was often the case.

Now my picture was splashed over their newspaper as a saviour, would I be seen as a marked woman by Mintoff and his merry men?

My movements were definitely restricted. One day I asked if I could go out to buy presents to take home but I was told if I wanted to go I would have to be accompanied by my burly minder.

I began to miss home dreadfully—and to wonder if I would ever see my family again.

The night before I left, under cover of darkness, I was taken to a smoky backroom in a casino where a dozen prosperous-looking men were waiting for me, looking expectant as I walked in with Dione and my ever-present minder. Their intentions became clear. . . they wanted advice from the Tarot cards! They urged me to ask the cards whether they should go ahead with plans to bring down Mintoff's government. I told them it would be foolish and they tutted impatiently. It was clear they wanted to take action now and the cards' answer was not what they wanted to hear. I told them they must exercise patience—there would be a new leader in Malta within the next three years. Despite their initial misgivings they accepted what I said. On 22 December 1984, exactly three years later, Mintoff had resigned. It was a noisy and unruly meeting. They shouted at each other—and me—in Maltese. But of course I hadn't a clue what they were saying. Not for the first time during my visit I wished I was anywhere on God's earth apart from Malta.

A few hours later it looked like I was on my way back home, my fears of being kept prisoner by Dione and his mob as their resident soothsayer having come to nothing. But my plane back to London was inexplicably delayed for an hour as we sat on the tarmac of the airfield.

Thoughts and deeds of the last week crowded my mind. I had a terrible feeling that someone was going to come for me and say: 'You're not getting out of this country lady!' Was I taking the Joan of Arc scenario too far?

I don't know—and to this day I still really don't know—what role I played in this Mediterranean political thriller. But one thing I do know. When we finally left the airport in Valletta and I stepped out onto British soil I felt immeasurable relief.

I may have changed the face of Maltese politics but it was good to be back in Glasgow knowing for certain that I'd rather be a housewife and mother—or even a clairvoyant—than a Joan of Arc!

Some time ago I was introduced to a middle Eastern

gentleman in London, Elisha, who was a director of one of the largest hotel groups in the world. He invited some friends and me to dinner at his flat the next evening. His flat, in the Knightsbridge area of London, was absolutely magnificent, abounding with flowers and priceless ornaments. We were received by the butler who travelled everywhere with his master!

After dinner I suggested I read my host's hand and as I didn't have Tarot cards with me I further suggested that if he put the white of an egg into a glass of water I could see what was happening from there. I started off by taking his hand and having a look at the lines. I could feel all his nervous energy circling around and I felt a bit dizzy. I asked him if he was occasionally bothered by dizziness and he confirmed that he had visited a clinic for tests for this very reason some days before. I also took a psychic pain across my chest and, yes, it was Elisha's pain—he had also had a cardiograph done when he was at the clinic, as he had been suffering from chest pains. I felt he had to rest more as his condition was mainly stress related. I went on to talk about his younger brother who had been drowned in America. Although this had happened about twenty years before, Elisha still bore a heavy burden of guilt for the accident. He later explained that he and his brother were playing on a canoe when it overturned. His brother was strapped into it in some way and got trapped under it while Elisha stood in a panic watching it going over a waterfall. A dreadful thing to have happened and to have experienced. I went on to give this charming man many details about his business which he agreed were spot on.

This was the first of many meetings with Elisha and soon he was organising me to fly down to London every other week to meet yet another group of his friends. He advised all his friends to write down what I told them and strike off each thing as it happened. Elisha had been doing this himself and most of what I had told him had already been struck off. After several months of travelling to London it was suggested that I might go out to Bahrain and work at the Hilton Hotel there, doing private consultations, giving talks on psychic powers and astrology and perhaps doing some readings in public by psychometry—holding an object that someone has been wearing and giving a reading by this means. I thought at first that this would be a great experience and spoke to some of my friends about it.

I went to see an agent in Glasgow called Tony Meehan who agreed to handle the contract for me. All seemed well until it became clear that our contacts in Bahrain didn't really know what was going on. Everything became a bit complicated. I eventually decided to pull out of the Bahrain trip when Tony received a telex asking him to state what mode of dress would be adopted by Darlinda, the belly dancer! I didn't think Bahrain was ready for this act just yet.

I have had a lot of contact with doctors, one way or another. Not only do I require them to look after my health but some of my best friends are in the medical profession! A close friend, Dr Sarah Marr, who is a general practitioner and broadcaster, suggested to her committee of the Johnstone and District Medical Association that I be the guest speaker at the Annual General Meeting. This was agreed although some of the other members of the association thought it was a bit unusual. After my initial talk on astrology and my unusual powers I went on to read the Tarot cards and then the hand of ophthalmologist Dr Max Nanjianni.

Max had always considered himself to be a Cancerian, born in July. However, one look at his hand told me he was a Gemini and must have been born in June. I told him so. Max was amazed and told the audience that his wife Edna had recently visited his sister from whom she learned that Max had been born in June and not in July as he had always thought!

I also do regular 'special events' for a variety of reasons.

My friend Janis Sue who owns *Signature Boutique* in Glasgow's exclusive Royal Exchange Square is always doing things for me. When I'm down she peps me up and when I'm ill she is almost like a nurse. Nothing is too difficult or too much trouble for her to do—for me or in fact anyone else. One evening she was having a late opening in the boutique to promote her gorgeous new collection, some of which had come from Germany and France. To thank her for all her support I suggested that I might come along and read dominoes for the customers. It sounded a great idea and would be lots of fun at the same time. Janis Sue and her staff were both delighted and excited. Janis Sue provided glasses of champagne and orange juice and a delicious buffet was prepared for the 'fun' evening. What transpired was not too much fun—it turned out to be rather serious. I used a set of rather lovely stone dominoes and the elegant ladies each took their turn sitting at a small round table.

I told a very serious looking lady that her husband was hiding something from her—it was news he had received in a letter, it would mean a change in his life style. Next morning Caroline told her husband over breakfast what I had said to her. He looked quite surprised and took a pause from eating his fried bacon, eggs, sausage, mushrooms and buttered toast etc. He then confessed to her that the week before he had received a letter from his doctor to say that his cholesterol level measured in a recent blood test was horrendously high and he had to adhere strictly to a fat-free diet. The two of them ended up in fits of laughter but that was the end of the fry-up breakfasts in the mornings. I'm delighted to say that his cholesterol level has now dropped considerably.

I told Jan, who works in television, about some glandular problems and this had just been confirmed on that very day by a visit to the hospital. I also told her that within a few days she would hear from a distance of the death of a man with the initial 'D'. Within the week Jan had heard of the death, in London, of a colleague, David Bell.

I told another lady that she was going to go on a wonderful trip on an ocean liner. She thought it unlikely as she didn't particularly like boats. She was surprised when she got home that evening to be told by her husband that to celebrate her fortieth birthday he had booked a flight to Florida and then a cruise on the 'Love boat' for two weeks. She sent me a lovely postcard saying how much they were enjoying themselves.

I told a rather sceptical lady about a theft and broken glass. When she got back to her car it had been broken into and the radio stolen. Broken glass was all around the car. She has asked me several times since how I could see things like this in the dominoes. I really don't know the answer to this myself. I too find it rather strange. I find that I can do readings from any object that I tune into. I often ask the person I am doing a reading for to put the white of an egg in a glass of water. It's quite amazing the shapes and the images that I can see in this. I even read a gin and tonic with a piece of lemon floating around in it at Heathrow airport one day. This was for my friend Nazy who caught me between flights and who was anxious about her future. Such is the life of an intrepid, roving clairvoyant!

Chapter 7
A DAY IN THE LIFE . . .

EVERYONE expects my life to be very different from theirs and it's not. I do get heavy demands made on me but who doesn't in one way or another? My phone at home never stops ringing—I have a business line and a personal line and often the two of them are ringing at the same time. As I write, the phone has rung and it was a happy father to tell me that my predictions were correct regarding his son and a court case: the son is now a free man. Such calls really make my day but often they are not so uplifting. Everyone thinks I have the answer to their problems and I wish I had. Sometimes friends phone me up and I find that by letting them tell me their problems it clears their minds and they solve their own dilemmas. This is the way in which all friends help one another. One time, my friend June's face kept going through my mind so I phoned her to ask what was wrong. In the image I had in my mind, she had tears running down her cheeks. She was delighted that I phoned. She had been just about to phone me as she was very upset having just had a row with a neighbour.

Sometimes I can sit and think about a particular person and within the hour they have received my thoughts and they phone me. Think of my savings in phone bills!

In a similar way of communicating, I often know when people who are miles away are in trouble or in an accident. One day while writing a chapter of this book, I kept seeing the face of Gary Thomson (of M & A Thomson, the publishers) going through my mind. His face seemed to be a bit swollen and I could see dark shadows around his eyes. This image recurred over several days and I eventually phoned his office in East Kilbride and was told by his father, Matt, that Gary had been in hospital that week having some back teeth out and, yes, his face was rather swollen and his eyes a bit black. Poor Gary—I'm glad to say that he's back to his handsome self again.

Sometimes I can actually feel the pain of someone else. Two weeks ago I had terrible pains in my stomach for no apparent reason. I got a phone call before lunchtime to tell me that my niece, Anne-Marie, had been in labour and had delivered her son Allan. Taking other people's pain is a very strange phenomenon and I can never explain to others exactly how it feels. Of course I know instinctively when something is wrong with Selina or Gary but I think this could be said of many mothers.

Needless to say, I don't have a 'typical' day, but then who does? Before I go to sleep at night I write a list of the various things I have to do the next day. My friend Anne Gibbons got me into this habit several years ago and I find it invaluable. If I don't accomplish the full list for the next day I have to carry the unaccomplished tasks forward to the following day and I don't allow myself to carry the list any further than Friday of that particular week. It's the only way I can get the numerous tasks done in my busy life. Normally, I get out of bed about 8.00 a.m. and stand under the shower for about five minutes to wake myself up and wash all the dreams of the night away. I then go into the kitchen, put on the kettle, give the cats milk and give two digestive biscuits to the dogs. I like to have noise around me so I usually put on the radio or the TV. Some mornings I'm in the mood for music. I love all types of music but especially classical. Mozart's *Sonata in C* is a favourite, particularly when my sister, Helena, plays it for me. On days when I feel down I listen to Vivaldi's *Four Seasons* and I am soon on top of the world again. I adore the new recording by Nigel Kennedy. Music definitely sets my moods. Next it's time to start on the various medicines that my body needs to keep it working. I prick my finger and put a drop of blood on a small plastic strip. This fits into a computer which measures my blood sugar. I then give myself an appropriate injection of insulin to keep my diabetes under control. Next I take my blood pressure and then jump on the scales to see if I'm retaining extra fluid or not. Then it's on to taking a selection of pills for my various ailments. All of this can take up to thirty minutes but it is all necessary to keep me alive so, of course, I don't mind! The injections continue throughout the day, before each meal, and mid-afternoon I have to take a measure of the wonder drug 'Cyclosporin' (or 'Sandimmun') which keeps my transplanted kidney in great working order. It is the most horrible liquid I have ever tasted, but it's bearable when added to a measure of *Irn Bru* which helps to kill the taste.

After all this I'm ready for something to eat. Usually I have a piece of wholemeal toast with *Flora* and some freshly squeezed orange juice. Decaffeinated coffee, about three cupfulls, is a must before I can manoeuvre.

My two German Shepherds gaze longingly at me, begging me to take them for their morning walk. It's the only exercise I have in the day so I spend about thirty minutes walking briskly. I really should try and take more exercise—next Monday I will make a determined effort to go to an exercise class!

By the time I return from the walk Dougie the postman has delivered my mountain of mail. Opening mail is one of my pet hates and always has been. I get all sorts of strange requests by post. I always expect the worst of sinister-looking envelopes!

I then take a look at my astrological chart and find

out if the planets are favourable for me or not that particular day. Fore-warned is fore-armed I suppose. I then meditate for about fifteen minutes to get myself into forward gear, strengthen my state of mind and eradicate fears.

At least one day a week I have to make my way to one of the various hospital clinics I attend.

On Monday mornings I am called by Lorna at West Sound at about 10.15 a.m. to speak on the Lou Grant show. This consists of a three-way conversation between me, Lou and one of the numerous people who have written in to him to have their Tarot cards read over the air. Lou is always kidding me on about my weight and often asks for the photograph that he says I promised him about five years ago, of me wearing a bikini. He then proceeds to ask me how many lunches and dinners I have attended in the last week, leaving no one in any doubt as to my likely shape in a bikini! Like many women I used to be always talking about diets, calories and losing weight. My friend Kitty who is a clever Gemini made a very sensible comment when she said, 'When someone meets you in the street they are not going to run up to you and lift you up and say, 'Wow, you feel six pounds lighter—well done!' These words have been going over and over in my mind and now I am convinced that I will just be happy weighing ten and a half stone. I know some people who have all the money they could possibly want and all they can talk about is their weight and how many calories they have cut out today—what a bore!

Lou is marvellous at promoting anything we are doing for the kidney treatment charity. He has a fabulous personality and a wonderfully quick sense of humour. After my part on the show, at 10.30, I start to write my Darlinda column for the *Sunday Mail*. I carefully look at how the planets are behaving and connecting with each of the twelve signs of the zodiac. I usually accomplish this over a period of about two days, or longer when I do the full page once a month for the *Sunday Mail* magazine.

If I'm at home for lunch I usually pop a 'Lean Cuisine' meal quickly into the microwave but more often I have to go out to lunch. *Dalmeny Park Hotel* or the *Waterside Inn*, both in Barrhead, are my favourite local places. If I have to go into town it's the *Ubiquitous Chip* or the *Rogano*—lunches are usually business meetings or meetings regarding the charity. I don't eat a lot for lunch but I do love soup so it's usually two courses and coffee—never a pudding. In the afternoon I try to get some more writing done but this is not easy as the phones never cease to ring. No matter how carefully I plan my day it never seems to follow the plan. Hardly a day passes without a frantic phone call from a friend who needs my help for one reason or another.

Some days I appear to be on a psychic high and all sorts of weird and wonderful things happen. I hear voices talking away to me and sometimes I am conscious of myself answering back. People look at me in a strange way when they hear me talking to myself.

One day in the lovely *Tinto Firs Hotel*, where I now consult on one day each week, I was on a particularly high high-day and the kettle in the room kept boiling. The first couple of times it happened, I just thought that I had had a slight lapse of memory and I had switched it on myself, but when it happened for the third time I knew that it wasn't all in my mind. I actually disconnected the plug and believe it or not it still went on to boil one more time. If I could manage to do this at home what a saving we would have on our electricity bills! I love working at the *Tinto Firs* as the staff are like one big happy family of which I am a part. The appointments there for this year have been booked since last April and

I have over 400 people waiting on the cancellation list.

Once a month I go to prison! I am a friend of the Special Unit at Barlinnie Prison in Glasgow. I was first introduced to it by my friend Larry Sullivan of radio and TV fame. Larry phoned me up one day and asked if I could do a special favour for her. As she has helped me in my charity work in numerous ways, I assured her that no matter what she asked me to do, I would agree to it. The Special Unit at Barlinnie Prison was set up in 1973. Its aim is to help difficult, long-term prisoners to come to terms with their sentences and to prepare for the future. It tries to achieve this by operating as a small self-regulating community, with every prisoner participating in its operation.

The last time Larry had visited the Special Unit an unusual request was made of her—could she arrange for the prisoners to meet me? I met Larry in the car park in front of the forbidding building, shaking slightly, I must admit, but wearing a bold, bright turquoise suit to give me confidence. We got a warm welcome from the guards who asked us to sign in and then a lady frisked us and told us to go into a waiting room.

Some other guards arrived and escorted us across to the famous Special Unit. There we found a lovely rose garden and a small aviary which houses a wee rabbit as well as the birds. We were taken up to see the 'rooms'. The cells don't have locks and every one is individually furnished, many full of the prisoner's own works of art. Some have fire surrounds with electric fires. Small ornaments, a plaque bearing the words 'The greatest dad in the world!', and similar paraphernalia adorn the mantelpieces. The single beds have cushions behind them and some have velvet bed ends. Most cells have carpets and rugs. Lots of people disagree with the existence of this Unit, but although these men are here for a reason and I deeply sympathise with the people and families they

100

have harmed, I feel that prisoners are already being punished by being kept away from their own families and loved ones. However that is just my opinion and I don't imagine that it will be shared by all. On that first visit a small man with bright eyes came excitedly to greet us. I thought he was another guard and asked him if he enjoyed his job. He quickly put me right by telling me he had been convicted of killing a man, with a further conviction for taking a shot at the 'polis'. I was stunned! How could such an apparently charming man do such things?

The other prisoners are all just as interesting. They each appear to have found some individual streak of talent while locked up for such a long time. One prisoner told me of how he felt the first day he was taken from D block and put into the S.U. He had been a hell-raiser and the authorities decided that giving him a term in the Unit might settle him and ease the problems he was causing. The first morning he had to make a decision about what he should have for his breakfast. He found it impossible to make the choice between porridge and an egg. All his decisions had been made for him in the decade he had spent 'inside'; he never had to think for himself over this period. This illustrates one of the ways in which the Special Unit tries to help men to take responsibility for themselves again.

Some time ago I was speaking to Sheila Davis who owns the Scottish Modelling Agency, and she asked to come along on one of my visits to the Special Unit.

So last week, when I was going to view an art exhibition there, I phoned Sheila to ask her if she would like to come along and she was delighted to do so. I think she was a bit frightened at first when we entered the doors of Barlinnie and were escorted to the Special Unit, but once we were inside she was quite amazed at what she saw, the roses were blooming in the garden, new baby

101

rabbits had been born and the birds were singing in the aviary. Everything was just so lovely, as lovely as it could be inside a prison. We met a few people inside and one of the prisoners showed us around and took us into a room which contained work done by the prisoners. Sheila didn't realise this man was a prisoner, she thought he was a guard. She asked him if he had done any of the work on show. He said that yes, he had done various things, and showed them to her. Sheila suggested that he get one of the barrows at Princes Square, the new and very select shopping area in the centre of Glasgow, and display his work as it was absolutely gorgeous. The man looked at her in complete astonishment. He probably would be in prison for many more years and not in a position to set up a wee barrow in Princes Square for some time to come! Later, we were taken up to one of the cells, where we sat chatting to five prisoners about everyday things. One of them asked us if we would like some tea. We accepted and were then offered ordinary tea or Earl Grey. We took the chance of some Earl Grey: civilised living indeed!

After we had had our tea, Sheila asked when we were going to meet the prisoners. She had no idea that we had just been sitting having tea with prisoners who were quite dangerous, or who had been quite dangerous at one time.

The only time I ever felt any fear in the Special Unit was at five minutes to five when one of the prisoners said 'If you don't get out of here for five o'clock you will have to wait until six thirty' and I suddenly thought 'Oh my God, now I know what it's like to be shut in somewhere and not to be free.' We got out with about thirty seconds to spare. 'Panic in Barlinnie.'

The last time I visited the Unit, Mark McManus of the successful TV serial, *Taggart*, was there too. The prisoners treat him with great respect. I wasn't quite sure if it was Mark they were speaking to or 'Detective Chief Inspector Taggart'. Mark gives a lot of his time to help the prisoners in this very Special Unit.

I try to have everything completed by about 6.30 p.m. as Rajan usually comes home from work in the hospital at about 7.30. I'm ashamed to say that dinner is usually a main course from *Marks and Spencers* with fresh fruit and vegetables. If we go out in the evening to eat it's usually Chinese at the *Ho Wong*, Italian at *Fazzi's* or an Indian at *Mother India*. Most evenings are taken up with either meeting friends socially or organising events relating to the charity.

I seem to have a very busy social life—sometimes *too* busy—but I do enjoy meeting and talking to people from all walks of life and am so lucky to have many good and generous friends. One special friend, who is, sadly, no longer with us, was Sir Hugh Fraser. He was a giant of a man and when he entered a room it took on a bright warm glow. He hated snobbery and always managed to bridge the gap between 'us' and 'them'. The apparent hothouse conditioning never rubbed off on him. He used to laugh and say that I was one of the few people in life who, like himself, were classless. I think that my schooling may have been responsible for this. We would often sit and talk about snobs and 'toffee nosed' people who annoyed both of us immensely. I first met Sir Hugh when I was about eighteen and working in Tony Gilmour's, the florist, in West Nile Street. I was asked to do some charity work. Along with some of the other florists, I went to a dance in the Central Hotel, which was lovely in those days, to sell single flowers for 10/- (or 50p) which in today's terms would be about £5.00, so you can see what a very grand occasion it was. These were to raise money for the Heart Foundation. Sir Hugh was there with his mother, Lady Fraser, and his father, the late Lord Fraser. I remember looking at him and thinking he had walked straight out of a film, he looked so handsome in his beautiful resplendent kilt. I next met him about fifteen years later at a horse show and his warm personality won over everyone in his company. He was a grossly misunderstood man—typical of his Sagittarius sign. He lived for today and to hell with tomorrow. He had great enthusiasm and really meant what he said. His Aquarian moon gave him clear humanitarian guidelines. He managed to translate everything he felt and envisaged into mental image. In this strange way he was able to identify with others. He had a very shy streak but loved to circulate and meet new people no matter what path in life they walked. He had a self pre-occupied arrogance with an eye to eye contact that sometimes unnerved people. He broke many hearts. Women fell over their own feet in the rush to meet him. He had a magnetic attraction and could laugh at himself and his gambling follies. He smoked from the time he was twelve and told me of how the chauffeur would come to collect him and he would 'borrow' a Woodbine and sit in comfort, in the back seat, smoking until he reached home. He was one of the kindest people I have ever met. He would often come along to my home, have a Bacardi and Coke and sit and chat to other visitors who had dropped in. One particular evening the ex-Tory M.P. for West Renfrewshire, Anna McCurley, happened to be visiting and he and Anna got involved in the topic of Scottish politics. Everyone there was amazed at just how much he knew about Scotland. He could talk well on just about any subject and always stuck up for the underdog. He couldn't abide to see suffering of any kind, especially if children were involved. No-one will ever know exactly how much of his own personal money he gave to the needy, but whatever has been published in the newspapers can be multiplied time and time again. He was always chasing rainbows and I am sure now he has found his pot of gold and will be happy and content for ever after. Everyone does get their rewards—sometimes not in this life!

However, back to today, and a glance at my diary tells me that on Tuesday we have arranged to meet our friends, Anna and Lawrie for dinner. I'm looking forward to that! Two of my colleagues from the *Sunday Mail* are visiting me for a vegetarian meal on Wednesday. Chairman of our charity Robert Kelly has organised a meeting for Thursday night to discuss the forthcoming *Dynasty Ball*, and Friday is a steak pie and peas evening at the home of a friend. Bed time is usually around midnight if we can manage it.

Chapter 8
ENCOUNTERS WITH STARS

I'm the one with the crystal ball!

ARIES (21 March to 19 April)

Ruled by Mars, Ariens are pretentious, positive, passionate, ready for action at all times and love to be in charge. They have great confidence in their own ideas and opinions, are superb organisers, skilful motivators and have the courage of their convictions. The mood of the Arien can change very quickly however—quiet as a lamb one minute and seconds later a rampaging ram. Ariens are bold, energetic lovers, can fall in love with the speed of light and fall out just as fast. They are not known for tact and diplomacy when it comes to hiding their true feelings.

Two of my favourite Ariens are Rikki Fulton and Peggy O'Keefe. Rikki is overflowing and brilliant; new ideas flood his mind constantly, he appears to know something about every subject that is mentioned. He is a wonderful pianist as well as an actor and comedian, although he can appear to be rather aloof at times and has some very direct opinions. He has the true Arien winning streak and never admits defeat. I first met Rikki about fourteen years ago at his luxurious home which he shares with his wife Kate. I never tire of watching my brother-in-law's video of *Scotch & Wry*.

Peggy O'Keefe is the most talented pianist I have ever met. Her sunshine smile and charm hypnotise everyone she meets. Peggy is always listening to others' problems and trying to put the world to rights. She was born in Australia and is always promising to go back there—but what a loss Glasgow would suffer if she ever does make the final decision. Poor Peggy is always being asked to help various charities and works endlessly for Renal Research (Western Infirmary) and also for the Heart Foundation. I don't think there is anyone in show business that Peggy doesn't know.

Edward Chisnell, Arien author of *The Bell and the Tree* and talented creator of the famous Glasgow posters has a flair for the supernatural which never ceases to amaze me. He has often tried to convince me that Frankenstein was a Glasgow man!

TAURUS (20 April to 20 May)

Ruled by Venus, the planet of love, harmony and beauty, Taureans are thoughtful, sexual and stand firm in their ideas. They tend to be conservative and resolute, love luxury and beautiful surroundings and enjoy trea-

108

sure hunting at jumble sales and in antique shops. Home is of the utmost importance to the Taurean and is always adorned with the best knick-knacks they can find. They love being in love (and make wonderful lovers!), but they don't take kindly to anyone trying to rock their security and can be defensive and dubious of other people. Great connoisseurs of food and wine, they have a tendency to put on some extra pounds, but their charm and charisma more than makes up for it.

Among the numerous Taureans I have met Joanna Lumley must be the most beautiful. She has the grace of a swan and, intellectually, is as sharp as a needle. She appears to have read every book and newspaper ever printed from cover to cover and is really well informed. She is extremely bright and with her brilliant brain she appears to have the gift of summing up any situation at a glance. Her energetic approach to life made me feel a shade dull and lazy. She was totally intrigued with what I told her.

William Roache or Ken Barlow of *Coronation Street* has a great interest in astrology himself. He has one of the most colourful auras I have ever seen and is very down-to-earth. He has an instinctive feel for reality and appears to be on the same astral plane as Prince Charles with respect to the positions of the earth and planets and the close emotional links with his family. His insight is penetrating, intense and accurate. I felt totally at ease in his company.

Another Taurean who impressed me greatly is Dr Mary Watson of the Renal Unit at Glasgow's Western Infirmary. Although Mary isn't a household name, she is the leading star at the Renal Clinic. She has a charisma that stretches out to everyone. She takes such time and has such patience even though she has to deal with dozens of patients every morning. She has a variety of 'one-liners' that can put awkward or nasty people in their place in a second. It's funny to watch how people juggle themselves around in the queue trying to get her attention, but all patients get the same care and consideration regardless of their status or position.

The *Eastenders* programme has quite a few Taurean characters. Pam St. Clements, who plays barmaid Pat Beale, is a very down-to-earth character with a cheerful smile which nevertheless hides all sorts of secrets. I found her very pleasant. Peter Dean who plays Pete Beale was fascinating. He was a joy to meet—a breezy, lively man whose expressive face conveys all the feelings of his heart and soul. He is deeply involved in Buddhism and has very strong healing powers.

Glasgow's most famous criminal lawyer, Joe Beltrami, is the gentleman I have to thank most of all for without him this book would not have come about. Joe epitomises the true Taurean character. The presence he creates and his 'larger-than-life' personality is so typical of his sign.

GEMINI
(21 May to 21 June)

Ruled by changeable Mercury, the messenger of the gods, those born under the twin sign of Gemini often seem to have two quite separate personalities. Sometimes, for example, they swing suddenly from being a congenial, fascinating and fun-loving companion to an aloof, sarcastic and sulky 'stick-in-the-mud'! Geminis are always talented, resourceful and adaptable. They have a grasshopper nature, seeming to change their personalities according to the situation or the people around them, but they are happiest as the centre of attraction. Geminis pay particular attention to detail and like to get to the root of the problem; they love reading and often turn out to be brilliant public speakers.

The twin personality of the Gemini can sometimes lead to deep inner conflict however: in love affairs, for example, they may find themselves having to make a difficult choice and Geminis often marry twice.

I always seem to be surrounded by Geminis in my life as many of my best friends were born under this complicated mercurial sign. I still have to meet a boring Gemini, they always have something interesting to say. TV presenter Paul Coia has lots of Gemini charm and Dougie Donnelly too is typical of this sign—he appears to be able to do six things at the same time. I met them both for the first time ten years ago and they still look exactly the same today. I think they must have discovered the secret of eternal youth! Perhaps they will write a book and let us all into their secret. I remember reading that Joan Collins, who was also born under this fun sign, owes her youthful looks and hour-glass figure to eating grapes and drinking champagne. I think I would tire of the grapes but champagne is another matter, isn't it?

Another famous Gemini is the Glasgow-born author Margaret Thomson Davis. I am a great admirer of her work—she is so talented she can actually make the characters in her books seem to come alive. When I read *Rag Woman, Rich Woman*, I was lost in the true Glasgow characters, so many of which seemed to be just like people I know. Reading her books helped me though my painful dialysis days.

Multi-talented Gerard Kelly, star of the TV programme *City Lights*, has definitely got two sides to his personality. He has insatiable curiosity and seems to overflow with energy. Although he has a lively sense of humour, he also has a serious side to his nature and worries a lot. I find him one of the funniest men on TV and he is always eager to give his help to charity work. Talking of charity work, one lady who comes all the way

Michelle Collins, who plays Cindy Beale in the TV programme Eastenders, *is an amusing, versatile and witty Gemini.*

from London to help raise money is Gemini Faith Brown. She sparkles with wit and good humour. Her hand is one of the most interesting I have ever read.

I met the Olympic swimmer Duncan Goodhew some years ago and he radiates with Gemini sex appeal. After meeting him I started going to the local baths again but I'm afraid I still can't swim. He is really proud of being a Gemini. I wonder what the other side of his character is like?

Dress designer Lex McFadyen overflows with new ideas. His roving mind is never still. He has created some of the most glamorous and unusual fashions I have ever seen. Lex was born just as the sun moved from Taurus into Gemini.

Singer Moira Anderson has a wonderful voice combined with a great sense of humour and unending curiosity. A warm and friendly person, she loves to chat and never appears to run out of words—she has a true

Gemini silver tongue and all the social graces.

Another Gemini singer, Calum Kennedy, used to have wonderful parties when he lived in his Elderslie mansion. There would be all sorts of entertaining people there and the evenings were enlivened with Scottish country dancing and, of course, wee drams! I love to hear his incredible voice.

CANCER (22 June to 22 July)

People born under Cancer, a water sign ruled by the waxing and waning moon, are often home loving and highly creative. Cancerians are defensive and like to hide behind their shells. They are never afraid of hard work. It's a patient, sentimental sign, very possessive and protective. Cancer is concerned with food, organisation, shelter, children and everything that is basic for human survival. They tend to hang on to all their yesterdays with love and sentiment. Living in the past is a big part of their make up, throwing away old photographs is impossible! The Cancerian moods fluctuate like the cycles of the moon itself, but in general they make fun out of the most difficult crisis—their sense of humour is never far away. Shrewd in business, they are renowned for loud emphases and are no softies when it comes to material wealth. They find it hard to let go after love affairs have ended. When a Cancerian is scorned then sweet charm turns to hurtful jealousy and the tongue is like a snake's, vindictive and spiteful.

I often meet singer Mary Sandeman at parties; she is a wonderful conversationalist and appears to know so many interesting things about Scotland. Mary has a public face but a private personality. She is very much in control of her emotions but always has a lovely smile on her face. Lots of famous dress designers like Pierre Cardin, Elizabeth Emanuel, Hardy Amies and Teddy

Tinling were born under this sign. Cancerians are dedicated followers of fashion. Princess Diana was born under the water sign.

Fiona Kennedy, whom I have known for several years, has a very special talent both in singing and in children's entertainment. She still looks as young now as she did when I first saw her at the age of twenty-one. She is a very strong-willed Cancerian who always manages to get her own way.

I have lots of Cancerian friends but I haven't met too many famous personalities under the crab sign.

LEO (23 July to 22 August)

Torrid, amorous and lavish describes the kings and queens of the jungle. They love attention and admiration and will go out of their way to get it. They like to be the boss because they feel no-one can compete with their expertise. They do work hard but are demanding and expect everyone to be fired with the unlimited energy they possess. They like to do things with 'pzazz' and make generous passionate lovers, but they do need lots of admiration and compliments. The female lion is cooler by nature and a bit more calculating but both have strong sex drives and warm hearts. Anything mundane or ordinary they find boring and are at their best using their creative and organisational skills.

Entertainer and television host, Allan Stewart, has been a close friend for many years. I never tire of listening to his chatter on or off stage. He has a larger than life personality and exhibits all his Leo pride. When I am ill Allan never fails to send me a cheery or cheeky 'get well' card.

Bright and bubby Elaine C. Smith is another Leo who brims over with enthusiasm. She seems to play ten different roles on the same day and plays each one

*Allan Stewart and I doing our thing at a function
to raise money for Kidney Research.*

equally well! Her adrenalin level is always high and often
makes me feel laid-back and lazy. She goes into raptures
when she talks about her beautiful daughter Kate.
Although she has had such wonderful success her two
feet are still firmly planted on the ground. Elaine's husband Bob shares my birthday on September 2nd.

115

Another Leo, Tony Bennett, has the most gorgeous eyes I have ever seen. Reading his hand was like studying a road map, it was full of interesting and intriguing aspects. He told me that I had discovered more about his dark secrets than anyone else. He sent me a lovely letter of thanks after our meeting.

Singer and lawyer Peter Morrison is one of my favourite tenors. I could listen to his wonderful voice for hours. It must be great to be so talented in two separate professions. Peter is always most friendly and polite.

I met actress Susan George when I appeared on the *Star Signs* television programme. Susan is as bright as the Leo sun itself and puts great enthusiasm into life. I was able to tell her lots of intimate details regarding her secret friendship with Prince Charles. She shares his love of horses.

I was particularly interested to meet actress Sue Lloyd as she has been a diabetic for the same length of time as I have. She is very philosophical about life. We had a long chat about our common complaint and also about her future.

VIRGO (23 August to 22 September)

Virgo is ruled by Mercury and Virgoans are fastidious, critical and earthy. They make great communicators, broadcasters and writers and they also do well in medicine. They tend to be fussy people—particularly when it comes to straightening pictures or picking crumbs from the carpet. They also seek perfection in relationships, always looking for the perfect partner and sometimes end up marrying later in life. They are a lot of fun and enjoy a good laugh. They live to please their partners and have a tendency to overindulge themselves. They are sincere people who can be relied upon in a crisis, although they do love to be the centre of attention and

116

some have even been known to fake illness to get noticed.

Being a Virgo myself I usually get on quite well with other fellow Virgoans. Larry Sullivan of radio and TV fame has been a supporting friend for many years. Pert and precise she oozes with fabulous personality. James Hunt the ex-racing driver is also a Virgo. He has a quite formidable physical presence and puts up a defensive exterior at first meeting. His Aquarian moon suggests he has high ideals and he has very strong feelings about what should and should not be done. He sees everything with great clarity but can be very secretive about his personal life. He has true film star looks and can charm the birds off the trees!

One Virgo I have never met (but it's one of my ambitions to do so) is Mother Teresa of Calcutta, I have enormous admiration for her. What an enthusiastic lady she is—she puts everyone in the shade and always gets her message across and things done. I wish I was a wee bit more like her.

LIBRA (23 September to 23 October)

Libra is ruled by Venus and people born under this sign are serene, sophisticated and affectionate. Libra is represented by the scales—but the scales of most Librans are often out of balance and their moods can change several times in the same day. They have a great thirst for knowledge and use their smooth tongues to get you round to their way of thinking. Librans are not the most domesticated of the signs but they do strive for harmony and beauty in their home surroundings. They love expensive clothes, are fastidious about their appearance and don't like to get their hands dirty. In emotional situations they can be rather detached until a special person comes along, then it's promises of undying love

117

forever. Laziness can be a tendency but so long as their surroundings are tidy they are quite happy. Prone to a sweet tooth they sometimes have some extra pounds to shed, and do enjoy the finer things in life.

Two years ago I was appearing on a charity show with two Libran footballers, Paul McStay of Celtic and Ally McCoist of Rangers, both of whom are so delightful and charming. I was reading out a questionnaire regarding the traits of those born under this sign and I said that Librans never tired of looking at their reflection in mirrors. Then I asked if they had lots of mirrors around the home. Ally quickly assured me that there was no room for mirrors on his walls as they were covered with photographs of himself! Not surprisingly he nearly brought the house down with laughter.

Libran Andy Cameron can be so serious off stage and so hilarious when on. He too is always willing to lend a hand when money is being raised for a needy charity. He is so typical of his sign as he appears to know something about everything. I would love to know where he gets the time to read as he is such a busy man—he seems to be here, there and everywhere at the same time and he never appears to run out of energy or information.

Eastenders star Sue Tully is a delight. She seems to overflow with natural charm. I was never particularly impressed when I saw her on TV but my impressions changed very quickly when I met her face to face. She is a wonderful person and has the good looks of the Libran—particularly her exceptionally beautiful eyes.

SCORPIO (24 October to 22 November)

Power-packed and passionate, that's Scorpio! Their charismatic smiles and penetrating gaze tend to leave you weak at the knees. Scorpions are totally trustworthy and good at keeping secrets although they are not concerned with idle gossip, nor do they suffer fools gladly and can be quite sarcastic. On the plus side they make loyal friends and take friendship very seriously. They enjoy being in charge and giving out the orders but usually are fair in their outlook. Their magnetic personality makes them popular with the opposite sex and although sex is very important they can easily keep their emotions separate.

One of Glasgow's famous dress designers, Moira Withers, who goes under the POD and JOIS labels brims with delightful Scorpio ideas. It's lovely to walk through the luxurious London stores and notice her labels on the beautiful and exotic gowns. I often go along to Moira when I am going to a special engagement and ask her to make me something that gives the impression I have lost a stone in weight—she never lets me down!

Scorpio comedian Johnny Beattie has helped me so much and in so many different ways. He is always there to offer the right advice and willing to help when I crawl along to ask for help just one more time when raising money for Kidney Research. He and Kitty Lamont (his wife and one of my best pals) have a really talented family and their two daughters are now actresses.

Dorothy Paul, an actress perhaps best known for her role in the hugely successful Glasgow play *The Steamie*, is an absolute delight but she is also a very spiritual person. Dorothy has a wonderful concept of life. I have often heard her saying that you should be careful of how you treat people on the way up as you may need them on the way back down. I remember Dorothy since her *One O'clock Gang* days, when she appeared with Larry Marshall, Charlie Sin and Peter Mallon.

The most aloof Scorpion I have ever met is actor Peter Cook. Previously when I watched him on TV I thought he was so funny and I admired his quick wit and satire, but when I actually met him I was unimpressed to say the least. When I spoke to him he answered in monosyllables and seemed to look right through me. I don't think I impressed him either—anyway as the saying goes 'you can't win them all'!

Sports commentator Archie McPherson has a tremendous personality, and is a typical Scorpio—straight-talking and direct but with loads of charm and sex-appeal!

SAGITTARIUS (23 November to 21 December)

The Sagittarian is direct, courageous, friendly and kind; loves to be loved, needs to be needed. Ruled by restless Jupiter they like to keep moving—even if it's only moving ideas around—and are always coming up with new schemes and ideas although they do have a tendency to get bored easily. They abound with energy and hate to feel restricted. Sagittarians make friends easily but like to have several strings to their bow, in fact a bit of a 'here today gone tomorrow' attitude. They don't take life too seriously, but can be a bit 'over the top' at times both verbally and in the things they do. They love to travel and enjoy sport. Fun is important and they are not the most sympathetic of people if you're feeling down. Generally intelligent people, they rarely reach their full potential intellectually.

The late Pat Phoenix or Elsie Tanner of *Coronation Street* was a versatile, open-minded Sagittarian; she always managed to find a silver lining behind the blackest clouds in her life. Her optimism seemed to spur on everyone around her, although she was a bit unrealistic at times. After I had read her hand and told her that she would marry again, she said that there would be no way that she would wear another wedding ring. I was delighted when I saw the photograph of her wedding in

Pat was a very psychic lady herself!

the newspapers just weeks before she died. Pat herself was very psychic—she read my hand and told me I was going to make a journey to Canada as she could see a big maple leaf on my hand. She was spot on, and later that year I did take the predicted journey. She also told me that I should have more confidence in myself—I'm still trying!

Two other Sagittarians I have met are Billy Connolly and Pamela Stephenson. I found them good company but both quite eccentric. Pamela sat and spoke to my 'other half' (who is a doctor) about medicine and her fears regarding the growing Aids epidemic. She is really well informed and appears to care deeply about what is happening in our world and how we can put things right.

Gregor Fisher, who plays Rab C. Nesbit in the popular *Naked Video* TV show, is as funny off screen as he is on. He was born just as the sun was leaving Sagittarius to move into Capricorn. Gregor is always intrigued to learn what the Tarot cards have to say to him. He is a bit psychic himself and often after I have given him a reading I see shadows of people who have moved on to another level all around him.

CAPRICORN (22 December to 20 January)

Prudent, cynical, painstakingly patient and with a rigid and conventional outlook on life—these are the typical characteristics of this sign. Capricorns hate change of any kind, are full of practical commonsense and make excellent breadwinners, although they can flirt outrageously when the mood takes them!

Capricorns have a strong sense of responsibility, they move slowly and methodically through life, working hard, looking out for opportunities to come their way, ready at all times for action and self-assertion. They are immensely serious people, make use of all their talents and learn from their mistakes. They may appear to hang back and let others walk in front of them—but the Capricorn will always get there first! They are good at giving and carrying out orders and can earn money in the most unusual ways. (Always be nice to a Capricorn as they are likely to be the boss one day!) Capricorns often find that true happiness does not come to them until later in life.

Capricorn has never been my favourite sign but I have managed to meet some delightful ones. I have been on two TV shows and several radio shows with Michael Aspel who has magical Capricorn charisma, he puts everyone at ease as soon as they meet him. He is a true professional and everything must be perfect before the show starts. I've never once seen him become irritable and he has the happy knack of smoothing over the gaps if one of his guests happens to lose their nerve. His wife, Liz, was really nice too and I had a great interest in what the future had to say for her.

When I was in my late teens I was arranging the flowers in Glasgow's Central Hotel and I got to know the singer Johnny Ray who was born in Oregon in 1927. I remember I volunteered to read his hand and he was so impressed that he sent me numerous cards from different places he visited. He also gave me an invitation to visit him in the States but it was never to be accepted—no it wasn't because he was a Capricorn.

Noel Young, editor of the *Sunday Mail*, is one of my favourite Capricorns. He has been a friend for many years and he has nine out of ten traits of this surefooted, cynical sign.

Sydney Devine, the country and western singer, is another Capricorn who is deeply attached to his traditional values. He has turned his ideas and talents into a wealthy business. Indeed, some of the world's wealthiest people turn out to be Capricorns.

Radio Clyde's Peter Mallon was also born under this musical sign. His glorious voice gets stronger as his hair gets whiter! Both Peter and his wife are really entertaining company.

One comedian who doesn't have to say anything to get laughs, is Capricorn Jack Milroy. I think Rikki Fulton and Jack playing Francie and Josie are the funniest act I have ever seen. Jack always has an interest in everyone and will always make time to say hello; this may be because he himself has been so ill that he knows what it is like to be 'on the other side of the fence'.

Jack and his wife, Mary, are two of the most delightful people I have ever met.

AQUARIUS (21 January to 19 February)

Extremely knowledgeable, friendly and original, but terribly unpredictable, that's Aquarius. The sparkling eyes and warm smile is a giveaway of the intellectual air sign. Sometimes they seem to feel the world owes them something, although they usually get what they want since they have the strongest will of all the signs of the zodiac! Aquarians have an insatiable thirst for knowledge—if there is something to be found out they are sure to find it, and, of course, they make wonderful detectives. A strong rebellious streak is always prominent. The free spirit of an Aquarian can never be captured. Their favourite party trick is to argue the opposite point of view whether they believe in it or not.

Marti Caine is one of the nicest Aquarians I have ever met. She is so down-to-earth that it becomes embarrassing at times. When I met her she was going through a horrendous time as her first husband had just left her and she was travelling around with a young gentleman companion with whom she didn't always see eye to eye. Her reading told her about the older man who would come into her life and there would be another marriage. It all looked as if it was happening very soon and, in fact, it did. The initials of the gentleman were spot on.

DJ Ken Bruce is a really interesting Aquarian. I was on every Tuesday with him on his programme from BBC Scotland for about six months. We would phone one of the 'superstars', having already worked out their astrological chart from their date and time of birth, and I would tell them about future events that would affect their lives. Ken was great to work with.

The man who is more like Robert Burns than Burns himself is John Cairney. He is also an Aquarian and is a brilliant actor. He always has some fascinating and amusing tales to tell at parties and is never lost for words. Russell Hunter, the actor, is another Aquarian I'm delighted to say I know. He is quite typical of his sign—definitely bizarre! He has a collection of the strangest objects ever to be seen.

Dot Cotton or June Brown is as complex in real life as she is in *Eastenders*. She has an intelligent, inquiring mind but, at the same time, has some deeply-held beliefs. She is a truly rebellious spirit although she doesn't expect too much from her emotions. A very dramatic lady.

Michael Bentine has one of the most psychic auras I have ever seen. I enjoyed talking to him when I had a meeting with him in Edinburgh one day. He is very knowledgeable about spiritual matters. He told me about numerous strange events he had experienced.

When I went along to visit the actor Christopher Biggins in London, I was absolutely overwhelmed by the fabulous atmosphere he has created in his opulent home. Chris is so talented and so caring. His personality seems to stretch for miles.

One of the artists I admire most in Glasgow is Lesley Main. I think her paintings are astonishingly beautiful and she has such a lively stimulating personality—a typical Aquarian!

PISCES (20 February to 20 March)

Seductive, secretive and sensitive, Pisceans are difficult to fathom out. Often they are a complete mystery to themselves and hate to admit it. The dreams and illusions of a Piscean have no bounds—they are as deep as the sea. Tears and laughter come easily to them—often both at the same time. Sometimes they seem not to like themselves very much, but this does not prevent them from spending lots of time wondering what is the best way to impress others. The symbol of the sign—the fish swimming in opposite directions—represents the two very different worlds that they live in; they can have a cruel streak but also an equally kind and giving streak which worries about the whole world. Sometimes they are more at ease with animals than with other human beings.

Harriet Buchan who plays the wheelchair-bound wife of Taggart, in the TV programme of the same name, is a very impressive lady. She is musical, artistic and is constantly on the search for perfect bliss. She always takes the time to listen to others' problems and gives constructive advice without actually interfering. I always think of her as the 'daffodil lady' because several times when I have been ill Harriet has appeared with an armful of daffodils to cheer me up.

Taggart, alias Mark McManus, is also a Piscean. He looks so serious on TV but he is really funny off stage. He had a group of us laughing until early morning one time we were up in Aberdeen doing a show for Grampian television. I seem to remember he was relating some weird and wonderful things that had happened to him when he was in Australia filming *Skippy the Kangaroo*.

Celtic Manager Billy McNeill is a Piscean with terrific strength and stamina; he always looks so calm and charming whenever I meet him. I last met him at the launching of lawyer Joe Beltrami's latest book.

It was a real joy to meet the late Kenneth Williams. He became an instant friend and was a great fellow. He was such a popular man—I was a guest at one of his birthday parties and was so impressed by the efforts each of his friends had made to bring him something special. He had a wonderful sense of humour and could easily switch from accent to accent. A true Piscean, facing up to reality was just not his style. He told me about the great bond he had with his mother—he found that he just couldn't bear to be separated from her for long. He really was a lovely man.

Chapter 9
SPIRITS, STONES AND
STRONG BELIEFS

O NE OF the questions I am asked from time to time
is 'Are you a spiritualist?' The answer to this is a
definite 'no' as I cannot contact people on the
'other side' when I try. Sometimes, however, people
who have died come to me unbidden. This usually happens when the person consulting me has strong psychic
powers (without knowing it) and simply uses me as a
kind of 'transmitter'. One day recently I was doing a
reading for a lady who had a lovely lilac-coloured aura
all around her. I was deep in concentration when I heard
a voice saying 'Tell Mary that it's me, Christine. I want
her to know that I'm really sorry about what happened at
Abigail's wedding.' I relayed the message and my client
turned very white. When she eventually spoke she said 'I
came here with an open mind. That was my Aunt Christine. She died at my daughter Abigail's wedding reception seven months ago.' I had to get the lady a cup of tea
to revive her—perhaps it should have been a whisky
(although on second thoughts the two spirits may not
have blended!)

Often a wee man from Larkhall comes through and
talks to me about his tomatoes—his name is Willie Anderson—no messages for anyone, it's only his tomatoes
that he's worried about.

A young girl I will not name, as her family are very
well known in Scotland, comes through to me often. She
took her own life about three years ago and she often
talks of how people and their lives are ruined by
ambition and greed and how some folk get their values

all wrong. She talks to me both about people I know and about people I have never met nor ever will—in this life anyway.

One morning in my office I was doing a reading for a lady when suddenly her husband, who had died six months before, came through. He had been an ardent gardener and had specialised in growing roses. He told me the name of the rose he had called after his wife and said it was a particular shade of silvery pink. The lady was taken aback. She told me all about 'her' rose. I felt as if the rose was in my hand but knew it was only a psychic rose, an imaginary one. As the lady left I noticed in the outer office, in a small vase on a coffee table there, the self-same silvery pink rose. Neither I nor my secretary could think of any logical explanation of how the rose could have got there, but it certainly wasn't an imaginary one this time. Valerie, from the office above, came down to confirm that it *was* there and that she could actually smell it. The rose lasted in all its glory for about four days until its petals fell and littered the table top. The aroma lasted until the petals were finally swept up and disposed of.

Not so long ago in a room of the *Tinto Firs Hotel*, where I sometimes consult, there was the shadowy figure of a boy sitting near to me on a bed and chatting away to me. The wee boy's name was Douglas and he had a mark across his lip. When my first client came in I asked her if she knew a small boy called Douglas, with a mark on his lip, who'd died. 'No,' she said, she didn't know anybody called Douglas. I felt a bit stupid but I asked the next lady the same question, had she known a small boy called Douglas, with a mark on his lip, who'd died? She said, 'Oh my God, that was my son.' He had died at the age of ten, while having an operation on his mouth.

I often go down to London to visit a friend, Nazy Cook, who owns some fashion boutiques. One evening we went out to *Groucho's Restaurant and Club* with some other friends of Nazy's. During dinner I looked down at my side and I could see the image of a German Shepherd dog. There was a strange atmosphere in the restaurant although it was busy with customers, some of them very recognisable, including Lenny Henry, Steven Fry and Jennifer Saunders. Obviously a very civilized place! I felt very uneasy during the meal and I asked the owner If I could go upstairs and have a look at the room above. I told him that I kept hearing the name Toni Parrachelli. The owner agreed and as we ventured up the stairs I could hear a lot of Italian-sounding voices. When he opened the door of the room above the restaurant I was horrified to see the ghost of a man lying in a pool of blood and I could hear the ghostly dog barking. The owner then told me that the building had previously been occupied by the Mafia and there had been many strange happenings there. One of those living there had a love of Alsatian (German Shepherd) dogs and there had been quite a few of them roaming around the building at that time. He advised me to go and chat to a gentleman who owned a coffee house called *Beritalias*. He would be able to tell us about the place, as he had been employed there at that time. The next night we went to *Beritalias* for coffee. The owner was rather hesitant at first but when Nazy told him of the strange feelings I had experienced the night before he said that the Mafia had run the place for about five years; a gentleman called Toni Parrachelli had been murdered there and one of his German Shepherd dogs had also been shot. Several people could hear the dog barking long after the building had been totally evacuated.

As I say, I don't know whether I believe in spiritualism or not. I don't understand it, but I do see 'shadows' and they talk to me from time to time.

My mother died ten years ago. She was well up until

nine weeks before she died, at the age of eighty-four.

My brother, her only son, died a few weeks before, on December 10th, her birthday. Although we didn't tell her, she knew. There were quite a few strange happenings just before her death. One Saturday afternoon, when she was lying ill in the bedroom upstairs, my sister Margaret Mary was sitting near the top of the stairway reading a book and listening in case my mum called for anything. I was downstairs with Selina when one of my zany friends, Betty Shulz, came in with her daughter Karen, to bring my mum some flowers. Suddenly we were all aware of a choir singing *How Great Thou Art*. The sound wasn't coming from the TV, which showed horse racing. I suggested that there must be a radio on upstairs and went out into the hallway to meet Margaret Mary coming down to see if we had a radio on downstairs. There was no radio on in the house. It was strange, but lovely. In the last two weeks of my mum's life we had to have a nurse in three nights a week and either I or one of my sisters would sit with mum as well.

One day after one of my 'nights on', exhausted, I was sleeping in the next room while a nurse and one of my sisters kept watch in mum's bedroom. In mum's room I had hung a mourning brooch which had been given to me by an aunt. It hung on a long chain. One side was jet inlaid with gold and pearls. The other held a small photo of me as a child. The brooch was hanging by its chain on the doorknob of the wardrobe opposite mum's bed; the jet side was towards the room, the photo flat against the wardrobe door.

Suddenly, in the silence of the sickroom, there was the sound of a single tap on wood. The watchers looked round to see what it was. The brooch was still hanging from its chain, but now the photo side was turned towards the room. They turned it round. Again it twisted back of its own accord, and this happened as often as they tried. It was as though even in sleep I was keeping an eye on my dear patient.

After my mother's death, whenever I wore the brooch I heard terrible noises of people moaning and I sweated buckets. I then started to have strange dreams, all in the brightest shade of emerald green. I always value myself at being able to interpret most dreams but these ones were beyond me. I remember in some of the dreams I was floating through lengthy corridors and trying to get through hospital doors—all painted green.

Only finally did I connect the dreams with the brooch which I decided to put away in a safe deposit box in my bank. The sweats and noises and dreams stopped immediately. Perhaps, on reflection, I was trying to bring my mum—Old Bridget—back to join us, I missed her so much.

One of my friends at that time, Marjorie Orr, told me about the Victorian mourning period. In Victorian society there were strict rules governing etiquette during periods of mourning, which themselves were sharply defined—three months for an aunt or uncle, nine months for a grandparent, and one year for a parent, a spouse or a child. I can understand the value in having a recognised period during which mourning the loss of a loved one is not only permitted but expected.

At the same time as I was having my terrible dreams, my niece Helen Carlin could hear all sorts of funny voices talking to her which would cause her to go chalk white with fear. I really don't think my mother wanted to leave us any more than we wanted her to go!

I am always aware of what I have said or done during an interview, even if I may sometimes have so little control over what I do say that I appear to ramble. Once I realised in a shocking instant that I had taken on the voice of a dead man. I stopped what I was saying in mid-sentence, excused myself to the shaken client, and went out to the loo to recover. Then I returned and started once again, in my own voice. I have an open mind on the subject of spiritualism, but I refuse to practise it. I deal only with living people with whom I can communicate direct. I have no wish to involve myself or my psychic force in anything I do not understand. I believe in astrological forces. I believe also that there are forces of other kinds, which I tend to leave well alone.

I was once offered a thousand pounds by a woman to put a spell on her husband to make him impotent, since he was having an affair. I refused. A friend of mine was having a terrible time in her marriage a little while ago and applied for a divorce. Unknown to her husband she left a ring in his car which she believed would hasten the divorce and bring him bad luck. Her divorce still is not through but the car hasn't run well since. Rings are funny things. One was sent to me once by someone living in England. I got very strange vibrations from it, so I put it away in a drawer. It promptly disappeared. A few days later it turned up in another drawer, badly damaged and out of shape. I got a jeweller to fix it and then gave it to a friend as a present. She broke her leg and gave me back the ring.

I have been consulted by many business people, trying to keep a step ahead of events. I have been able to help countless people in this way. However, I have never been able to use it for self-seeking motives. It just never works as I learned many, many years ago—before I knew better. In fact anyone who uses clairvoyance or 'sending out vibes' for the wrong purposes will get their come-uppance and more.

If you are able to send out good vibes, do so. If you know someone who is feeling ill or down, get some of your friends to join in. Suggest a specific time—perhaps 10 p.m. each evening and get everyone to sit in their respective homes or wherever they are at that particular time, and start sending good healing vibes. I say a prayer when I am sending mine. It's really amazing how well it works. Everyone did it for me when I was ill and awaiting my transplant. I have started numerous groups doing good in this way. To do it you just sit quietly for a few minutes and get a picture of the person you are sending the vibes to in your mind and really wish them well. Often people come to me and ask me to help in such 'absent healing' for people I don't even know. To do this I usually obtain a photograph of the ill person and, holding the photograph in my hand, I send them out good vibes and ask God to help them.

A few years ago I was told about a wee girl of six called Karen who was ill in Yorkhill Hospital with a serious kidney complaint. I asked her aunt to get me some photographs of her and I requested various friends to sit and send loving, healing vibes every night at ten o'clock. Within a period of about six weeks Karen was feeling much better and was out of hospital. The growth that had been originally feared had disappeared completely. I know you must all be wondering that if this can happen for other people why can't I make it happen for myself? Although I have had diabetes and various other complaints, I have never been lying ill in my bed for long. When I feel ill my crystal is well used (of which more later), my friends and family start saying prayers, and I am well in no time at all, ready to fight the next battle. It's amazingly effective.

I am a great believer in healing crystals. I had heard of them through one of my dress-designer friends, John Ross, who was working in Los Angeles at the time. He had spoken to me when he was back in Glasgow on holiday and knew that I wasn't too well. Soon after, he came across some crystals in a shop and kindly bought me a lovely rose one. It took me some time to get used to using it, but it's absolutely magic now. I keep the crystal on the windowsill of my sitting room, reflecting the sunlight. It always looks interesting and bright and is packed full of healing energy and positive healing powers. Over the years it has helped all sorts of people, with both physical and emotional problems.

One lady who was terribly bothered with nerves and depression was told about my crystal by a mutual friend who had been helped by it to rid herself of headaches. I explained how the crystal is used and she managed to get her husband to bring her one from London. It was a lovely quartz one. Betty had prayed in her earlier days, but thought God didn't listen to her, as her wee boy had died of leukaemia. Anyway, she decided she would have another go. It was difficult for Betty to concentrate in the beginning, but after a while it became very easy. She sat cross-legged on the floor, said her wee prayer and got on with her concentration. It was almost like meditation, but only took about ten minutes of her busy time. Within a month she was back to her happy carefree self and had rid herself of her depression. Her doctor was really amazed at her recovery. After a few months she was able to discontinue her Valium, which she had taken for four years.

If someone asks for help regarding a particular problem, I usually talk to them at first about anything that comes into my mind, in order to relax them. I then talk to them about their particular problem or ailment and then explain how we are going to solve it. I believe that everyone has a certain amount of healing power. It's the most natural thing in the world for a mother to put her hands over a child's head after a bump has occurred. That's the mother using her 'healing powers'. If a person needs help because of headaches ask them to sit comfortably on a chair, put your hands over his or her head and ask God to help get rid of it. He's always around and usually helps. I used to think that he was some sort of smug and superior being, who wore a crown and sat on a royal chair up in Heaven. Now I don't think this is the case at all. He appears to be all around just looking for someone to help.

'Are you a healer?' is a question I am often asked. I don't think I am one of the world's leading healers, but it works when I try. As I said, most people have some degree of healing powers if they just try to use them.

I have a grasshopper mind that jumps from one thing to another. It is difficult for me to stay on one train of thought for long, as my mind wanders all over the place. I am also an optimist and rarely feel down for too long. My mother always said 'Laugh and the world laughs with you, cry and you cry alone.' These words are so true, and have been shown to be so time and time again.

People often ask me what an aura is and what colour is their aura? Auras are visible energy fields that surround every living creature and plant. When a photograph is taken by Kirlian photography (a form of photography used in connection with acupuncture and cancer diagnosis as well as parapsychology) the energy that surrounds a figure is shown in colour. The colour usually extends about a foot beyond the figure and depends very much on the individual's health and mood. The colour can change several times depending on what the person is talking about and if they are, for example, excited or scared. Gold to tan is a warm aura and means the person is easy to get along with. Orange denotes that they have lots of energy, but are perhaps a little nervous. If the person has a bright yellow aura they are generally highly intellectual. Blue is a cool aura—usually that of someone who is deep and has painted a veneer around himself or herself. Purple and violet suggest psychic ability and usually the ability to heal. Green indicates a well balanced personality and red is the aura of sexuality. If I am at a party and I see someone's aura turn a bright shade of scarlet it's because they have been attracted to someone across the room and if that particular person's aura turns the same shade it's heigh-ho and the two people are together before the evening's over. If I see someone whose aura is mottled, usually they aren't feeling too well or are perhaps worried. Mixed auras are occasionally visible, and possibly that individual is quite happy, although they may have some pain somewhere. Their aura will be gold with perhaps shades of pink, but around the area of pain there will be some grey-black or brown steaks. The nicest aura of all is pink, particularly if it is a deep shade. I usually notice this colour surrounding bridal parties.

I use colours a lot in my work. There is a colour associated with each Sun sign of the zodiac. Aries— red; Taurus— shades of the woodlands and country; Gemini— sizzling yellow; Cancer— strong blues; Leo— shades of the sun and gold; Virgo— either grey or navy and white; Libra— all sweet pea shades; Scorpio— blood red and maroon; Sagittarius— purple and royal blue; Capricorn— black and turquoise; Aquarius— air-force blue; Pisces— all shades of the sea.

When I really want something important to happen I try to make it happen and this works, nine times out of ten. Colours can come into this too. If I want to solve a problem I concentrate on the colours amethyst or violet and the answer I am looking for comes very soon. When I'm feeling low I look hard at a piece of bright yellow material and I'm soon feeling up and full of beans again. I always surround myself with colour. Sometimes I'm sure I must look like someone who has escaped from an explosion in a paint factory!

People ask me if the colours they wear can affect their luck and they definitely can. How so? One of my friends, Frieda, wears all the colours of the rainbow and she always looks bright and happy.

People often ask me what their lucky colour is. As I have explained on page 138, certain colours are connected with each astrological sign. In addition, some people build up an affinity with a certain colour quite accidentally. Perhaps they were wearing blue when they received some wonderful news and ever since have believed blue to be lucky for them. If they believe it to be so then it probably will be! Conversely if a person was perhaps driving a red car when involved in an accident that person may came to regard red as an unlucky colour for them. The person may feel unlucky whenever she wears that colour and this may influence the outcome of things.

'What do you think of lucky charms?' is another question I am often asked. I have several charms that I have been given over the years and I would never part with them. I received a lucky teddy bear, with a red and white waistcoat, from my friend Kay several years ago, and it always sits on my bed. (I am a bit of a looney and I often talk to it!) The day I was given it I won a bottle of whisky in a raffle and the next Monday a letter came bearing the glad tidings of a small win on the pools, so it's definitely a lucky bear. I also have a polished stone, which came from Aviemore, and I always carry it in my bag. I think that if I happened to lose my bag it would be the losing of my stone that would upset me most! What I believe is that if you feel something is lucky then it usually is.

Mind over matter is something I firmly believe in. If you can manage to get yourself in a positive state of mind you will be surprised by the outcome of many of your worries. Take twenty minutes of your time and think of all the energy that surrounds us—we are all capable of tapping into the vast amount of unused energies that are free to us—it is all around just waiting to be used. Lots of people I have spoken to over the years have said that they find it impossible to meditate. They don't realise that deep day dreaming is a form of meditation and we are all quite capable (or guilty!) of this. The catch is that if you day dream or worry in a negative frame of mind it's more than likely that you will get a negative result. When I'm feeling low I sit in a quiet room and visualise what I actually want to happen. If I'm feeling poorly I visualise myself walking with a smile along a long country road with my two dogs. After a while my pain fades and I am feeling much stronger. If I want the outcome of a certain worry to be good, I visualise a big Christmas tree and I meditate on the shining star at the top and not on the branches sweeping out onto the floor at the bottom. Nine times out of ten the outcome is just as I wished.

This sort of relaxation can also be used in a panic attack, which I am very prone to. When I have an attack I take the telephone off the hook, sit on a comfortable chair, and stroke one of my animals. On many occasions I end up with my dogs and my cats surrounding me— animals are so sensitive to moods that they know when we need a little bit of help. This is mental first-aid and it's so easy to administer. By sitting quietly and concentrating on good health the body is encouraged to manufacture the necessary chemicals needed for mental and physical well-being.

A gentleman I know had suffered migraine for many years, but at first he pooh-poohed my advice about healing and the crystals. I am delighted to say that although not entirely cured he now only suffers from the appalling migraine on a few occasions a year rather than every other week. Even when he does suffer now the headaches are not nearly so severe or long lasting. He says he simply 'wills' them away and it's so successful. This is definitely a case of mind over matter, in which I am a great believer.

Laughter is also a great therapy. Perhaps one of the hardest things to learn in life is to be able to laugh at yourself. Once you have accomplished this, life and living become much happier and easier. There are so many people around who are so concerned with self that they are totally afraid to laugh in case they fracture their image, so allowing people to see beyond their façade. I really enjoy letting my hair down and going wild. I am just so delighted that I am still with you here on Earth. I may shudder to think of what people may be saying about me after a great party, but then I think back to what Oscar Wilde said, 'There is only one thing in the world worse than being talked about, and that is not being talked about.' He makes me feel better. So many people have forgotten what it's like to behave as they would really like. Life is to be enjoyed—it really costs nothing to laugh. Constant smiles and laughter help to keep your own chin up and convey happiness: a bit like sunshine. Always have a sunny look on your face—even when it's raining. If you are determined to win someone over, give them a nice warm smile—not just from the mouth, make sure your eyes sparkle—and the deal will be done. I hate to see people who smile and their eyes remain quite expressionless—they usually have empty, cold hearts and their eyes tell the tale. The whole body reacts to smiles and laughter. The magic of it can overcome most setbacks and can make making friends so much easier.

So many people make themselves ill or more ill than they really are because they feel so sorry for themselves. The 'Why me?' attitude. Doctors can often tell by a person's general attitude and frame of mind if they are going to make it or not. Those with a positive frame of mind can often make a good recovery while those who have a negative attitude may go downhill.

People often ask me about mind out of body experiences and I have heard of some weird and wonderful experiences that others have had. One such experience of my own happened in the mid 70's. I was at a social gathering where I met the chaplain of Strathclyde University at that time, the Rev. Max McGee. He was talking about mind out of body experiences and asked me if I had ever had such a thing. My answer was a sort of no–yes as I wasn't quite sure if I had or hadn't. Anyway, he took hold of both my hands and asked me to think of someone I would like to help. Into my mind came an image of the daughter of one of my friends. Her name is Caroline Smith and she had been in a wheelchair since babyhood. In fact I seemed to be on a plane going to America in which Caroline was walking up and down the aisle. The picture was very clear. She wore a brown skirt and a cream blouse. Her lovely blonde hair was cascading down over her shoulders and she had a beautiful smile on her face. Her walking came without any support or effort. I looked down from one of the plane's windows and I could see the Statue of Liberty in the New York harbour. I decided that the plane should turn back at this point as I didn't really want to land in America: it did turn. On my journey back I spoke to several other passengers on the same flight. One of them was a lady I used to know when I worked in the Inland Revenue. She had died the year before. Her name was Jenny Gillan and she told me about her new 'life' and about some of the interesting people she had met.

A gentleman called George Brunton, from Newcastle, was also on the flight. He told me he was looking for his daughter who had run away to America, to be married, after having an argument with her mother. About three months later I happened to meet this George Brunton at a friend's dinner party and he told the company about his daughter Gillian having had an argument with his wife, Margaret, and leaving Newcastle the following week to meet up with her boyfriend who was in New York. She subsequently married him.

When I was on the astral journey I was conscious of the three other people in the room with Max McGee, I could hear what they were saying and I was telling them what was going on in the plane. When I tried to get back off the plane and into my natural state I found it very difficult and this was quite terrifying. I made it though!

Chapter 10
WHY NOT TRY THE TAROT?

THERE is much speculation about the origins of the Tarot but its invention has been attributed to the Egyptians, the Chinese and the Indians. France claims to be the country through which it was first introduced to Europe. When you buy your first pack, and a pack of Tarot cards can be bought in most bookshops of reasonable size, handle the Tarots frequently to get the vibrations flowing between the cards and yourself. Don't allow anyone else to touch them unless you are doing a reading. The cards should be wrapped in a silk scarf or cloth and kept in a wooden box—this protects them from outside influences. For laying out the Tarots a wooden table is best, covered with a piece of silk.

There are many different designs of Tarots. One of my favourite packs is the one which was used in the James Bond film *Live and Let Die*. It is very colourful and it was this that first attracted me to it. But when I started to use the cards I got strong vibrations from them and I always have good results with them. The Magician especially seems to be able to tell me exactly what I want to know, and he appears at the right time too. I also use the Rider–Waite pack, whose designs, and particularly the beautiful pastel shades of the Aquarian deck, I love. The card eight, Strength, is significant for me, and when it comes up for myself I always know I will be able to overcome any obstacles in my way in the near future. The Empress in the pack usually signifies myself. I get great results from this pack, especially when I am in a pensive mood. In addition, in recent years I have become well acquainted with the Tarot of the Cat People. I find these cards both beautiful and fascinating. The backing on each of these cards shows two cats with eyes just like our own cat, 'Charlie'. There is at least one cat depicted on each card and I feel a great affinity with them.

The Aleister Crowley Thoth pack is a strange one. The cards themselves are works of art, each one taken from actual paintings done by Lady Frieda Harris, the wife of a prominent Member of Parliament at the time. She based them on sketches and interpretations given to her by Crowley and the originals are now in the Warburg Institute. Crowley was deeply involved in witchcraft. Every detail in the cards is symbolic of something related to witchcraft and black magic, and there is also an astrological connection in each one.

The first time I saw this pack I was immediately apprehensive. The cards seemed to emanate evil, and after handling them I had to wash my hands to try and get rid of the bad vibrations I was sensing. My hands would actually jump up and down whenever I came near them afterwards. One day, on holiday, I needed to compare some cards in the Crowley pack with those in others. Selina was with me in the room and as I put out the cards we both saw out of the corner of our eyes a sudden movement. We looked towards it. On the mantelpiece my wristwatch, which I had put there for the time being, was rocking back and forth of its own accord. I am sure it was the power of the cards. I haven't touched them since.

There are seventy-eight cards in the complete Tarot pack.

Divination through the Tarot

There are various methods of practising divination, or prediction, through the Tarot. I do however find something I call 'Darlinda's Christmas Tree' to be the most successful and revealing spread. The interpretations are related to the cards and vary depending on whether a card falls the right way up or in reverse.

The procedure for doing the Christmas Tree spread is relatively simple. After the client has shuffled the cards, take them and spread them face down in a straight line or semi-circle, whichever you prefer. Ask your client to pick any thirteen cards. These cards should then be handed to you. Lay them face up on the table, making the shape of a Christmas Tree. Start with the card at the top and then put one down on each side. Repeat this until you have just two cards lefts. Put these two in the middle—the tree trunk. The diagram below illustrates the sequence clearly.

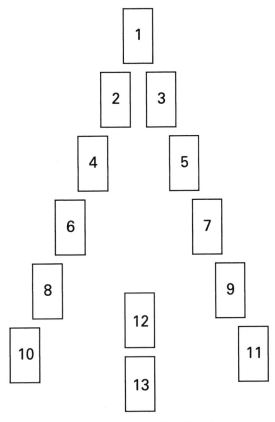

Darlinda's Christmas Tree Spread.

When interpreting the Tarot, always bear in mind that the cards near or on either side of a particular card in a spread do relate to it. A few examples of this are given on page 171.

Once you have done the Tarot a few times you may find that you 'feel' or say certain things that are not associated with the cards on display. Don't repress this; on the contrary, encourage it. This is your psychic ability being developed through the Tarot and is part of the process. Now for the meaning of each card.

The Major Arcana is the most important part of the Tarot and represents events in the near future. The Minor Arcana represents events which will occur further ahead.

First we will look at the cards of the Major Arcana. Remember that the meaning of each card is dependent upon whether the card is in the upright or the reverse position.

The Major Arcana consists of twenty-two cards, and the Minor Arcana of fifty-six cards. The Major Arcana comprises individual cards while the Minor Arcana is divided into four groups. These groups, or suits, are associated with the ordinary playing cards we use today. In the Tarot, the suit of Wands is equivalent to Clubs, Cups to Hearts, Swords to Spades and Pentacles to Diamonds.

Each suit is connected with a different area of life:

Wands	Reputation, fame, enterprise and efficiency
Cups	Love, happiness, harmony and unity
Swords	Hostility, struggle, bitterness and malice
Pentacles	Money and material interests

It is significant therefore when many cards of the same suit turn up in a spread.

The Minor Arcana also contains Court cards. They are the King, Queen, Knight and Page of each suit.

THE MAJOR ARCANA

The Fool
A choice must be made. The carefree young man in the card with the dog at his feet and a rose in his hand, sails through life oblivious to problems. A time for facing up to reality. If in the upright position it is more than likely that the correct choice will be made.

If it comes in reverse, the wrong choices might be made, so be careful.

The Magician
This is the card of opportunity. You have the ability to get on in life so use it. You know what you want, so go out and get it. Remember, obstacles are there to be overcome. This can be the start of a new chapter.

However, in reverse the magician warns against the misuse of power, when plans could fail.

The High Priestess
Can represent deception—something is going on behind your back that you don't know about. Don't trust just anyone. Pick with care those you confide in.

If in reverse, beware of a strong and ruthless female.

The Empress

The card of fruition, fertility and abundance. Could be news of a birth. A pregnancy possibly to the enquirer. Material gains you are expecting will be greater than anticipated.

In reverse, expect emotional disharmony. This can also indicate a woman obsessed with becoming pregnant.

The Emperor

This is the card of leadership and authority. A man with great knowledge will give you some helpful advice which should be taken seriously. This person will hold a position of authority, or may be a father figure.

If in reverse, this card indicates a tendency towards weakness of character and possibly a fear of breaking free of parental influence.

The Hierophant

This card is closely linked with religion, morals and, sometimes, marriage. It may indicate a new look at religion and can mean a possible marriage. You will go all out to impress someone new who enters your life.

In reverse, you may be too superstitious at times and will not accept useful advice which will be offered to you.

The Lovers

Someone is attracted to you—a new love affair will start. It can also signify a business partnership if a card of the Suit of Wands is nearby.

In reverse, romantic disappointment is in store. The temptation to become unfaithful to your present partner may be strong.

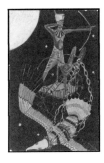

The Chariot

Can mean you are being pulled in two directions—take care over the decisions you make. Can also mean triumph and recognition in something you have been working towards.

In reverse, this card foretells of reckless actions which may result in losses. Triumph over rivals is also indicated but this will be obtained by unscrupulous methods.

Justice

The correct balance in life will be found. In legal matters, justice will be done.

In reverse, any dealings with the law will not turn out as desired or expected. Events will be hampered by the unfavourable attitudes of others involved.

The Hermit

A need to change course in life and rethink your plans. You may move away from home to do this. Long overdue character-building will take place. Final decisions will be your own responsibility. This card often signifies self.

In reverse, at times you can be your own worst enemy. Take care not to ignore sound advice.

Wheel of Fortune

Indicates great success in all your ideas and good fortune in money matters. Be prepared to take a gamble. This is the time to look for new opportunities and it could be for the best if you try something different. Life in general is getting better.

If this card is in reverse, it could be indicative of an unlucky gamble. Don't leave anything to chance.

Strength

You will have the courage to carry out any plans you have in mind. Don't be afraid to reorganise your tactics as this will meet with success.

If in reverse, the card of strength indicates that you will be less able to deal with problems as they arise. Beware, you could be taken advantage of.

The Hangman
You must face up to life's realities. Beware of becoming too selfish. Respect the wishes of those around you. Unexpected changes will take place on the domestic scene.

In reverse, be less concerned with yourself and more alert to the needs of others—very much the same as in the upright position.

Death
A frightening card to those who don't understand the Tarot. Only very rarely does it indicate death in the true sense. It usually signifies the end of one thing and the beginning of another.

In reverse, it means a time of inactivity and may mean trouble in government matters.

Temperance
A need for moderation. Try to maintain an element of balance in your life. Major decisions should be shelved until you are positive of the outcome. A need for patience to be exercised.

In reverse, although your difficulties may seem insurmountable, all that is required is organisation. In reverse this card also indicates unprofitable associations so it would be unwise to accept an offer of business partnership.

153

The Devil

A strongly sensual card indicating physical passion which could get out of hand. Beware of allowing physical inclinations to dominate your life. You many encounter a strong influence which should be resisted. This is also a card of restriction.

In reverse, the Devil card indicates that you will successfully overcome the less noble side of your character. Release from oppressive forces is also indicated.

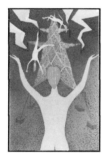

The Tower

The worst card in the pack. Indicates collapse or ruin, either at home or of unfulfilled plans. Can indicate imprisonment. Also appears when a person is at his or her lowest ebb, when everything has gone wrong for them.

Unfortunately, in reverse, the indications are very much the same.

The Star

The star of hope. Great improvements to your present position are indicated. I feel quite happy when this card appears.

In reverse, you experience uncertainty and have a negative outlook. You should try to combat these.

The Moon
This card warns of deception and changes beyond your control. Can mean depression, but most of this is now in the past—you will come through it relatively unaffected.

In reverse, a similar interpretation though less negative. You will be forewarned of the dangers and deception indicated. Concern yourself only with the practical matters of life.

The Sun
A great card, indicating success and achievement. This discounts the bad influences of negative cards in the spread. Indicates happiness and good health. A new venture will be successful.

In reverse, there may be irritating delays to plans and failure to attain goals but try again.

Judgement
Release from past worries. The trial is over. Relief from responsibilities. Good things will start to happen, so be prepared for sudden changes for the better.

In reverse, there are still certain trials to be gone through in life. Periods of hope will bring respite from worry but do not become complacent. More effort is required in the solving of problems.

155

The World
Successful completion of plans and projects. Others will rely on you when you make important decisions. There will be extra responsibilities which you'll be able to cope with. This is the best card in the whole pack.

If the world is in reverse all is not lost, but you may have a little longer to wait for all you desire. Persevere.

THE MINOR ARCANA

Suit of Wands or **Suit of Batons**
(reputation, fame, enterprise and efficiency)

Ace
New beginnings which will bring changes to your way of life, particularly in your career. A birth to a member of the family or someone close. An important communication will be received.

In reverse, delays in business plans, a relationship may not lead to marriage or the permanence you desire, difficulty in a desired pregnancy.

Two
Success will come through determination. Talks will take place which may result in a partnership of some kind. Your signature will be required on a document which will bring you future security.

In reverse, not a good time to put business ideas into operation. Be patient, put more thought into plans and discuss carefully with others involved.

Three

Look for the right person to give you assistance in any project which is important to you. Anything new which you begin should prosper.

In reverse, an unavoidable change of plans, unforeseen circumstances will cause delays.

Four

You'll be more than satisfied with the results of past efforts. A time of peace and harmony. Romance, or possibly marriage, is indicated.

Even in reverse this card brings good tidings but to a lesser degree.

Five

Pressures could become intolerable. Now is the time to stand up for what you believe is right. Quarrels are indicated. The cooperation you require is there, but the whole truth must be told.

In reverse, the meaning is similar but more serious—a law suit could result.

Six

You can expect good news to reach you so don't give up now—keep trying and success is assured. Relationships all round will get better.

In reverse, not a good time to carry out certain plans. Another's victory may be your loss.

Seven

You will battle against the odds. Take a break from your everyday routine and you will find the answer to your problems. This is a time for holding on—not giving in—and you will come out winning.

In reverse, people around you will try to take advantage of you. Guard against indecision or you could lose out on opportunities.

Eight

Your affairs will undergo major changes as a result of news you receive. A journey could be made in connection with career matters. Your financial position may be reorganised. A new idea could produce excellent results.

In reverse, a domestic upheaval is foreseen. Also, bad news concerning a business venture.

Nine

Persevere with an idea but listen to advice given by others. You have come so far but you don't have all the answers so heed what others say, but don't give up what you have already achieved.

In reverse, past pressures have taken their toll—you are feeling weakened by them. This could be self-inflicted, however, and it's time to examine your inner self.

Ten

This is not a nice card either way up! It indicates that the failure of plans is likely and you will have to accept this and start afresh.

In reverse, someone will try to place their burdens on your shoulders. Do everything in your power to resist this as it will be most unfair.

Suit of Cups
(love, happiness, harmony, and unity)

Ace

Domestic affairs are changing for the better. A change of residence or changes concerning your present home. You'll be strongly attracted to a member of the opposite sex who enters your life. This is an excellent card for romance and health. Lots of love surrounds you.

In reverse, the happiness you seek will come, but you will have to wait for it.

Two

The beginning of a wonderful new love affair or friendship. You'll receive cooperation from someone who will help you reach your goals. You can look forward to a surprise communication which will make you happy. Can denote a proposal of marriage

In reverse, there will be setbacks in a romantic relationship, but these won't result in a final break.

Three

This card indicates a gathering of people and there will be much rejoicing. It could also indicate a completely new lifestyle. News of a pregnancy for yourself or someone close. Can also indicate a marriage is near.

In reverse, changes are indicated but plans won't work out as you had hoped.

Four

You'll be unhappy and bored with your circumstances. A 'couldn't care less' attitude is evident and no one appears to understand your feelings. You'll also be emotionally discontented. The time has come to think about what you really want out of life.

In reverse, you may misjudge a newcomer—don't be too trusting.

Five

A marriage or partnership looks set to break up. It's time to think carefully before reaching decisions. Could indicate difficult times for a loved one.

In reverse, this card shows that all is not lost.

Six

Old friends or associates will come back into your life. An opportunity to change jobs. You could receive an inheritance which will be full of surprises. A new friend comes into your life.

In reverse, the six of cups shows that you tend to cling too much to the past, refusing to let go. It's time to face life as it really is.

Seven

A very difficult decision is in front of you, but there appear to be many options open to you. Use logic and common sense—you know what must be done, so do it. You are on the verge of a new life cycle.

In reverse, not a good time for you just now. Any small successes should be followed up.

Eight

Boredom and dissatisfaction. Your plans are not progressing quickly enough. You may decide to try something completely different.

In reverse, disillusionment with the emotional side of life. Disappointments are likely.

Nine

This is the 'wishing card'. You'll feel in tip-top condition, due to improving health. Problems will be overcome or simply disappear. A favourable card for both emotional joy and material gain. This is perhaps my favourite card.

In reverse, unfortunately, the opposite. Your wish will not be granted. Also, you should guard against overindulgence in food or drink.

Ten

Sudden changes will bring you more happiness than you realised possible. Denotes a marriage and achievement of personal goals and dreams. A journey will have pleasant results.

In reverse, disharmony in the family. May also indicate damage to the home, e.g. a break-in.

Suit of Swords
(hostility, struggle, bitterness and malice)

Ace
Indicates the start of something you may be pushed into and this will not be to your liking. Something new may end in sorrow.

In reverse, beware of attempting to gain too much power over anyone or anything as you will meet with great obstacles.

Two
Many decisions are about to be made, but it won't be easy choosing the direction to follow. You will have to be firm with yourself.

In reverse, beware of making the wrong decision regarding a journey. Dishonour will come to a member of the family.

Three
Quarrels within the family circle which could lead to an eventual separation. News of a miscarriage.

In reverse, still the same bad news but not necessarily happening to you.

Four
Illness of someone close to you. (Illness to you only if coming next to Ace of Cups). Think carefully and don't rush into any new situations. Prepare yourself for changes that will inevitably take place, and don't be afraid to lay the foundations for future plans.

In reverse, caution is required before proceeding with any plans in mind.

Five
Failure and defeat in a project you had high hopes for.

In reverse, it foretells misfortune for a friend.

161

Six

You are coming to the end of a difficult period which has sapped your strength. You are on the road to happiness and contentment. A long journey across water is indicated.

In reverse, there is no immediate remedy to your problems. It can also mean bad news from abroad.

Seven

Your plans will suffer setbacks and won't materialise as well as hoped. Much of this will be beyond your control and it may be wise to change course and look for other alternatives. Don't attempt to take anything dishonestly.

In reverse, much better, something you thought was lost forever will turn up again.

Eight

Don't try to solve your problems alone. You are unable to make constructive decisions on your own, so seek advice. Certain restrictions or obligations could cause you to worry a lot. Your health is below par.

In reverse, someone you trust will betray you.

Nine

Look at the cards surrounding this one. The whole could indicate a serious illness to someone close. Unhappy news coming.

In reverse, a time for patience. You may have some trouble with nerves.

Ten

Unfulfilled plans and sadness for a close one. Depression and unhappiness at present circumstances. Your plans could fail and this will be difficult to understand. A separation within the family and a journey across water is indicated. A legal matter will dominate your thoughts.

In reverse, nothing worse can happen to you so it is time to turn over a few pages in the book of life, and start afresh.

Suit of Pentacles
(money and material matters)

Ace
An important document or other form of communication will be a basis for new beginnings. Most of your affairs look set for improvement. A legal matter will work out to your advantage.

In reverse, take care, great plans will not work out and you could lose money.

Two
Delightful news can be expected. Changes taking place will leave you with more than one alternative, but it will be in your best interests if you make your mind up one way or another. Be wary of people who try to put you off. Good news from overseas.

In reverse, you are having difficulty in handling some problems. Plans you have made will go wrong.

Three
At last your ability will be recognised and your efforts rewarded. Your financial position will improve. A large organisation will play an important part in your affairs.

In reverse, not a good time to ask your bank manager for a loan!

Four
The tables are turning. You'll soon be in command and able to do what you feel is best. Make a decision regarding finance, it should prove beneficial. You'll receive a gift.

In reverse, this card signifies loss of earthly possessions. In business, be very careful regarding money—a loss may be inevitable. Delays and obstacles may hamper business.

Five

You are on the threshold of accomplishing something important, so don't give in now. A legal situation could depress you, resulting in possible loss. Look after your health, the indications suggest you are neglecting it.

In reverse, a temporary job. You may also take a real interest in spiritual matters.

Six

Plans and hopes will begin to show improvement. Opportunities will come for promotion or other changes which will improve your financial position.

In reverse, beware: someone is very jealous of you and will try to do you harm.

Seven

Have patience now, for unexpected changes will improve your income. Plan carefully when making important decisions—not a good time for taking chances. Discussions will turn out satisfactorily.

In reverse, although you have worked hard there will be little to show for it.

Eight

Persevere with an idea, it could lead to you learning a new skill. You may have problems with cash at present, but a steady improvement is on the way. There is likely to be an opportunity to change your job or profession.

In reverse, keep plodding on with your job even if it's not as interesting as you would like it to be.

Nine

You'll achieve your material goals but don't work for them at the expense of emotional security. An abundance of money will never replace love and happiness—attempt to strike a balance. An enjoyable journey is in the offing.

In reverse, beware of legal entanglements regarding your home. Move with caution in everything you do.

Ten
Most of your affairs are improving. You'll gain financially or attain a higher position at work through the recognition of your abilities. An emotional problem is well on its way towards a satisfactory conclusion—but be patient. You may be buying some new property.

In reverse, watch out for problems to do with property: you may have to seek legal advice.

THE COURT CARDS

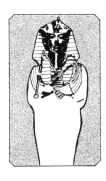

King of Wands
A settled man with country connections. A businessman who will give you sound advice.

In reverse, an uncompromising type of person who could cause you trouble and should not be trusted too much.

Queen of Wands
This card represents a woman in her maturity who is willing to give you assistance. She has a strong personality and is sensible, but you will have to approach her, she won't come to you.

In reverse, a strict and domineering woman but with a kind streak. Probably red- or fair-haired. She could be the instigator of deceit and infidelity.

Knight of Wands
A young man will put ideas into your head in connection with business. Something new starting. Possible change of residence or long journey.

In reverse, much reorganisation at work which may not suit you. Rely on your own efforts to gain information, not rumours.

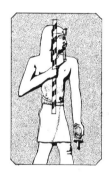

Page of Wands
News will reach you of a young, fair-haired person.

In reverse, there could be bad news concerning a young person. The surrounding cards will give some indication of whether the news is good or bad.

King of Cups
Someone, mature and respected, whom you'll be able to confide in and trust, will recommend what your future plans should be. Could be an unemotional man connected with the legal profession.

In reverse, someone you have always held in high esteem will be involved in a scandal that will shock you.

Queen of Cups

A warm-hearted woman will have the answers to matters which are causing you concern. She may give the impression of being rather aloof, but she can be approached.

In reverse, a lady who is too soft-hearted at times. A friendship with her could become quite bitter in time.

Knight of Cups

An important message coming from someone you love. A partner or some-one close could prove difficult when they oppose you for some reason.

In reverse, someone you trust will tell you a downright lie which will cause a lot of trouble.

Page of Cups

News of a birth to a close friend or member of the family. This card signi-fies a young person who can help you. A new idea can be developed.

In reverse, a warning of a miscar-riage or abortion.

167

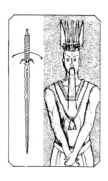

King of Swords

A reliable man who will be invaluable when advice is needed. This man does not commit himself before thinking carefully—he may be associated with the government or legal profession.

In reverse, a cruel and selfish man who always gets what he wants in the end. Take care.

Queen of Swords

A mature woman with a dry sense of humour can help you. Her financial position is strong. You may find it difficult to put up with present circumstances—she could assist you.

In reverse, a deceitful lady looking for revenge. Not to be trusted, she will do you harm.

Knight of Swords

Difficult times are being experienced. Look to a young man to guide you. This person may be rather forward but he will do everything in his power to protect you.

In reverse, a troublemaker who will start a dispute with you over a triviality.

Page of Swords

You'll be disappointed at the intentions and behaviour of a young person, usually with brown hair or eyes. He or she could force you to change plans and your relationship could deteriorate.

In reverse, be prepared for the unexpected. There is a possibility of ill health for someone close.

King of Pentacles

This is a reliable, steady and mature man. He is both friendly and clever and has a mathematical brain. Could be associated with property or banking. He will help you if you ask.

In reverse, a greedy man who is over-materialistic. Beware of bribery.

Queen of Pentacles

This card indicates a talented lady who has very strong family ties but is also good in business. Can be off-hand or moody. She could help you or someone close.

In reverse, don't trust this lady too much as her gain could be your loss.

Knight of Pentacles
Represents a young man who often gives the wrong impression but can be trusted. He will never try anything new unless he is absolutely sure it will work. He could waste much of his time and talents. He is always sympathetic to those less fortunate than he is.

In reverse, you must have more patience and guard against carelessness.

Page of Pentacles
A clever young person will be the bearer of good news. Changes are indicated due to the efforts of others.

In reverse, unfavourable news will put a damper on your high hopes.

When doing a reading pay attention to the group of cards chosen as a whole. Try to base your interpretation not just on individual cards but on the group, as meanings can be clearer this way. Look, in particular, at cards occurring side by side when laid out. Here are a few examples of interpretations showing the influence that one card can have on another.

Four of Swords/Knight of Wands
Think very carefully when someone comes to you with an idea. If you take the necessary precautions you should be successful. A journey will be discussed relating to your future plans.

The Empress/Page of Cups
Indicates a pregnancy for a young member of the family or close friend. Material matters will improve.

Five of Wands/Five of Swords
Certain aspects of your life are proving difficult. This could result in a break in a personal relationship. Do what you believe is right.

Ten of Pentacles/Nine of Cups
Be patient, most areas of your life are improving. Your problems will soon be overcome. Career and emotional matters are well on their way towards a satisfactory conclusion.

Ace of Wands/Six of Pentacles
You could receive an important communication that will bring improvements to your career. Finance is also favoured.

The Sun/Ace of Cups
Happiness due to changing domestic circumstances. The health of yourself or a close one will improve. A change of house is indicated.

The process may seem complicated but with a little practice all will become clear! To help you along the way, on the next page is an illustration of a Christmas Tree spread. See what you can make of it. My interpretations are given on page 173.

The World

Ace
of Cups

The
Tower
(Reverse)

Three
of
Cups

Four
of
Swords

Six
of
Swords

Queen
of
Cups
(Reverse)

Ace
of
Batons

The Hermit

Four
of
Pentacles
(Reverse)

Page
of
Wands
(Reverse)

The Star

Nine
of
Cups

The top card in the layout shown, the World, is the finest card of the Tarot and signifies that everything will eventually work out in your favour even if the other cards are less certain or are worrying. The World is a card of strength and courage. Next comes the Ace of Cups so a lot of love surrounds you, and as the three of Cups follows there will be news of a marriage, engagement, birth or celebration.

The four of Swords next to the Tower, which is in reverse, denotes news of an illness—as the Queen of Cups accompanies it a lady will be involved.

Be careful of money matters when the four of Pentacles is present—even in reverse. Nine of Cups is the wishing card so everything should work out as planned. On the other side of the spread is the six of Swords next to the Ace of Batons, which indicates a journey, and the Page of Wands brings news of the destination. The Hermit and the Star indicate that there is need for a change of direction in life and only you can make the particular change. As it is next to the Star there will be great improvements in your life: in general the Star can signify great hope when it comes in this position.

Chapter 11
PREDICTION WITH PLAYING CARDS

THE MODERN version of playing cards is derived from the Minor Arcana of the Tarot.

There are many methods you can use when foretelling the future with ordinary playing cards and when giving a reading it is indeed rare to stick to one particular method on its own. For myself, I have obtained the best results by using the following methods integrated into one reading. Your psychic ability should not be stifled when you are confronted with a client from whom you suddenly receive 'feelings'. On the contrary, it should be used in conjunction with the cards as they fall.

It is most important to put the person for whom you are doing the reading at ease and a warm friendly smile takes a lot of beating. Try it—it will probably even help you to relax too.

First, shuffle the whole pack yourself, making sure that neither you nor your client can see the 'faces' of the cards. Now ask your client to do likewise. Then take the cards and spread them on the table, face down, in a semicircle. Now ask your client to pick thirteen cards and once he or she has done so, take the remainder and put them to one side. Taking the thirteen cards from your client, you now lay them out one by one and read them in conjunction with your interpretations. Always remember that the card preceding or following a particular card will in all probability be connected with it in some way.

When this has been done, put the whole pack of fifty-two cards together again and shuffle them. From now on you are the only one allowed to 'mix' the cards. Now ask your client to pick any five cards. Take the five cards and turn them face up, one at a time, explaining the significance of each. Again the card preceding or following another card will be connected with it. Take the whole pack once more, shuffle it and ask your client to cut the pack into three. Turn up each set and read the three top cards, following the rule about the card before and after. For the final time shuffle the cards again and ask your client to cut the pack in half. This is probably the most important move of all. Turn each half face up. Here lies the final outcome of most of their hopes and wishes, the obstacles they will encounter and the probable answer to help them overcome these.

Please try this system. It works for me so there is no reason why it should not work for you.

CLUBS

Ace   Illness (if followed by a heart card it is in the family circle; if not, it is just someone you will hear of).

King   A dark friendly man will lend you a helping hand, just when you need it most.

Queen   A warm-hearted dark woman will be very helpful. You can put your trust in her.

Jack   A dark young man who is rather confused will be in your company. Try to make him feel at ease.

Ten   News will come about a legacy, or money from an unexpected source.

Nine   This usually means that widowhood will come in later years.

Eight	An invitation will come which you will consider twice before accepting.
Seven	You will sign your name to an important document. Take legal or professional advice if you have any doubts.
Six	A new friend will come into your circle and should be welcomed with open arms.
Five	News will come from abroad and you may have to read between the lines a little.
Four	A friend may let you down regarding a promise made previously. Find out why, for there could be a good reason.
Three	News of a temporary illness of a young person.
Two	You will be involved in a depressing matter. Don't keep it to yourself.

HEARTS

Ace	Romantic harmony will be restored in a previously disrupted atmosphere.
King	A fair gentleman with loving thoughts for you. His identity, when revealed, will surprise you.
Queen	A fair woman who is faithful and friendly. This person could do you a lot of good.
Jack	A fair newcomer coming into your life—don't be too sure of him as he may be over-charming.
Ten	Success in a love affair or happiness in marriage.
Nine	You're sure to get your greatest wish in life, but it may take some time to materialise. Be patient.

Eight	A light-hearted outing is ahead. One person you meet in particular could become a life-long friend.
Seven	Contentment in your home life, but effort will be needed if it is to remain this way.
Six	Good news regarding a child, possibly an achievement he or she has recently made.
Five	An invitation with a romantic link. You'll hesitate before accepting, but go ahead with confidence.
Four	You have a great love of beauty, art or music and will strive to surround yourself with such works.
Three	Too many people depend on you. Let others shoulder the burden for a change.
Two	Two big love affairs in life.

DIAMONDS

Ace	Something important regarding money is ahead. If followed by a heart card it is always good. If it is a spade it is not so good.
King	A man of power and strength will be contacting you. Money will be important to him.
Queen	A hard-hearted woman is around. Don't trust her.
Jack	A gentleman in uniform. Questions will be asked.
Ten	Money changing hands. Make sure you are in control of the situation.
Nine	A new business will bloom, but be prepared for extra work.
Eight	A short journey with a benefit at the end.

Seven	News of a job. Prepare yourself for a change.
Six	An unexpected gift will come your way.
Five	Be careful not to lose something of value, especially if a spade card follows.
Four	A fair man could ask you for a loan of something. Make sure you know exactly what is involved.
Three	A disappointment regarding a journey, especially when a club card follows.
Two	Two marriages when ace of hearts follows.

SPADES

Ace	When facing up, you will hear of a birth; when down, you will hear of a death.
King	A legal matter has to be considered and a dark gentleman will be involved.
Queen	A lady who is not to be trusted will come along. Watch out for her. Appearances will be deceptive.
Jack	A dark, devious young man could cause you trouble.
Ten	Worry will be sparked off by news you receive, possibly through a third party.
Nine	News of misfortune will come and your assistance will be required.
Eight	Tears of anger and frustration. Try to keep your temper in check.
Seven	Angry words with someone who is not related to you. Be very careful of what you say.
Six	News will come by telephone from an unexpected source.

179

Five	Cross words in the family if followed by a heart card—a rift could be created.
Four	News of someone who used to be in your life.
Three	You will mistrust a close one because of their strange behaviour.
Two	Be careful of an accident.

Here are a few sample interpretations showing how important the cards which precede and follow a particular card turn out to be.

If the spread of cards consists of the Queen of Diamonds, the seven of Clubs and the ten of Spades, you should be careful of a hard-hearted and domineering woman whom you talk to. She will try to force you into signing your name to a document and if caution is not exercised it will lead to worrying news at a later date.

If the spread of cards consists of the six of Diamonds, the King of Hearts, and the five of Hearts, then you can be sure that a fair gentleman who has loving thoughts about you will come to you with an unexpected gift. This will only be the beginning, however, as he is almost certain to follow this up with a romantic invitation. If this should be followed by the ten of Hearts then in all probability he will be the man you will eventually marry.

When the two of Hearts and the two of Diamonds are cut together, this means you will marry twice during your life and you will meet your second partner while still married to the first. The two of Diamonds and Ace of Hearts together also indicates two marriages. If the nine of Spades and Ace of Hearts are followed by the two of Diamonds, it means you will remarry after being widowed. You will receive money if the ten of Diamonds and Ace of Diamonds are turned up and the number of the card which follows will tell you how long you have to wait, e.g. a six—six days, weeks, months, or years. If one of the news cards appears such as the six or nine of Spades, the previous cards will tell you approximately when you will receive the communication and the first face card which follows indicates who it will come from, e.g. the King of Clubs—a dark, friendly man.

Chapter 12
TRY YOUR HAND AT PALMISTRY

PALMISTRY is one of the most popular methods of character analysis and personal prediction. The art of reading palms is attributed originally to the Chinese and the Indians around 3000BC. Much later Aristotle instructed Alexander the Great in its practice. And it is still used today.

I have read almost every conceivable kind of hand—including those of actors, authors, mountain climbers, businessmen, sportsmen, housewives and disc jockeys. My most unusual experience, however, was with a woman who appeared in my office with a small dog under her arm. She sat down in the chair opposite me and when I asked her to put out her hand, she said, 'Oh, no. It's not for me. It's for the dog.' After a stunned and speechless pause I did what she wanted. To my surprise I learned quite a lot from studying the paw of the little dog—its pedigree, its health and its chances of being a mother, with a suitable partner of course!

Some people prefer to do readings from a print of the hand rather than from the hand itself. In many cases the lines of the palm come out more clearly this way. To make a hand print you need—

1 A tube of finger print ink
2 A smooth surface (metal or glass) on which to roll out the ink
3 A roller of hard rubber such as is sold by photographic supply companies
4 A glossy paper

Squeeze some ink on to the glass or metal. Push the roller back and forth on the surface until the roller has an even coating of ink. Roll the roller over the hand to be printed. Place a piece of the paper on a soft or rubbery surface and carefully put the hand to it, pressing gently. Then roll the hand off the paper towards the edge of the hand so that the edge as well as the palm is printed. If you want the outline of the hand, draw round it with a pencil before the hand is lifted off. The ink is easily removed from the hand with a commercial hand cleaner. An alternative to ink is to make a hand print using an ordinary photocopier. This works surprisingly well!

There are no two hands (or presumably paws) exactly the same, and this is one reason why no two people's lives follow exactly the same path, or even pattern. It is not just the lines that matter—the shape and size of the hand itself, and the fingers, nails and thumbs, are important. The six basic types of hand can in themselves tell a great deal about the person for a start.

1   *The Elementary Hand*
    This type of hand tends to be on the clumsy side and the fingers are short in comparison with the palm. People with such a hand lack patience and quickly lose their tempers. They are also very passionate.

2   *The Square Hand*
    This belongs to a very logical individual who is a creature of habit and is always prepared to help others.

3   *The Spatulate Hand*
    The hand and fingers represent a fan. This indicates a restless, excitable person who goes to extremes.

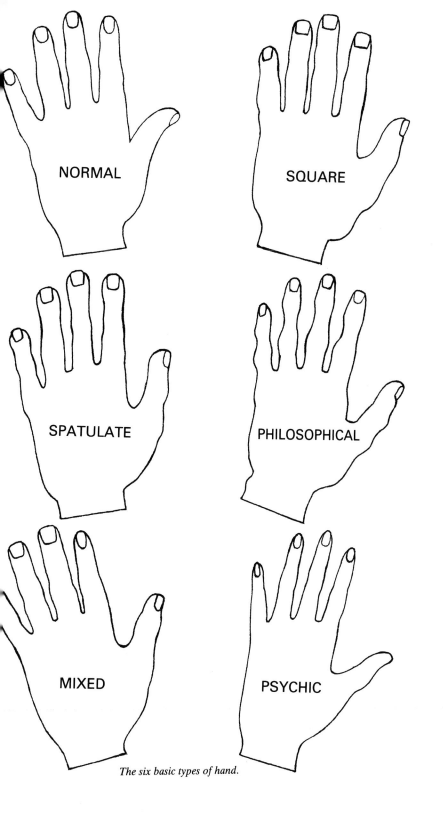

The six basic types of hand.

4   *The Philosophical Hand*
Many teachers, philosophers and intellectuals possess this narrow, pale type of hand. They are forever seeking the truth.

5   *The Mixed Hand*
This hand is neither one thing nor the other. It is a mixture. Even the fingers are of different shapes and this signifies that the person is very adaptable.

6   *The Pointed or Psychic Hand*
A long, narrow hand is prominent. The person is intuitive and follows his or her instincts.

Each finger is named, as follows, the relative sizes of the fingers giving an indication of principal characteristics:

First finger	Jupiter. Ambition, expansion.
Second finger	Saturn. Judgement, knowledge.
Third finger	Apollo. Exploits, achievements.
Fourth finger	Mercury. Observation, perception.

Long fingers
Signify the person is a perfectionist.

Extra-long fingers
Prone to exaggeration.

Short fingers
A very impatient person.

Nails

Short	Over-fussy and critical.
Narrow	Devious and secretive.
Ridged	Ill health in later life.
Wedge	Over-sensitive and moody.
Wide	Forward and go-ahead.

186

Thumbs (Shape)

Flat	Excellent with money.
Spatulate	Impatient but artistic.
Pointed	Jumps to conclusions—strong ideals.
Square	Logical and practical.

I take a reading from a client's left hand, and begin by outlining the most prominent features. The nine mounts of the palm are as significant as the lines, and signify not only abilities, characteristics and emotional tendencies, but also opportunities to come. The more prominent the particular mount, the more significance it has, and the greater its influence. It would need a whole book to describe all that may be seen in a palm, and the meaning of each sign. In this short chapter, however, it may be sufficient to say that in the same way that the mounts vary in prominence, so do the lines. In addition, the lines may start at and end at different points in a hand, and may be broken. For example, if the health line is broken, the subject could face an operation or serious illness.

Normally the left hand is used. Do not, by the way, take any scars into account. Nor is it advisable to read the palm of anyone too young.

To me, contact with the person through their hand is very important. When I take it I can tell if the person is nervous or has healing powers, just from the feeling that passes between us on contact. And I am often at my closest to them at this point.

THE MOUNTS

Venus
Venus is the sign of love and beauty and is associated with the astrological signs of Taurus and Libra. If this mount is well-developed it indicates a warm and sym-

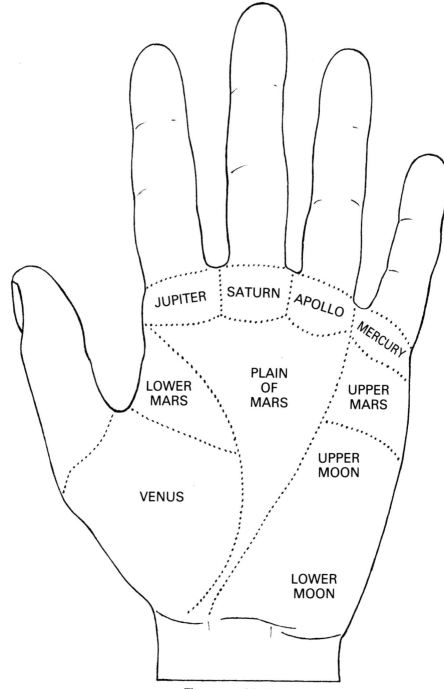

The mounts of the hand.

188

pathetic personality. It also denotes a very flirtatious character who desires to be loved both emotionally and sexually.

Mars

Mars is a war-like planet, full of energy. It is the ruler of Aries. If this mount is well-developed it shows great courage and strength. If the mount is flat there will be frustration and moods.

Jupiter

If this mount is full and strong there will be lots of luck and prosperity. Jupiter governs the easy-going sign of Sagittarius. Professional gamblers usually have very strong mounts of Jupiter. When this mount is over-developed, it is an indication of a great desire for power—Hitler's mount of Jupiter was like this.

Saturn

A fatty or well-developed mount of Saturn indicates someone who doesn't openly show affection. There is anxiety about security. Such a person often marries for security.

Sun or Apollo

A well-developed Sun mount indicates someone who is out to woo and win. They are great lovers of beauty. Rejection of any kind cannot be handled. They are inclined to be overpowering and can be showoffs.

Mercury

Quick wit and charm are indicated by a prominent mount of Mercury; however if this mount is over-developed the person can be overpowering and arrogant. These people never stay still for long.

Moon

This mount is associated with romance and moods. If over-developed it denotes someone who is indecisive and unrealistic.

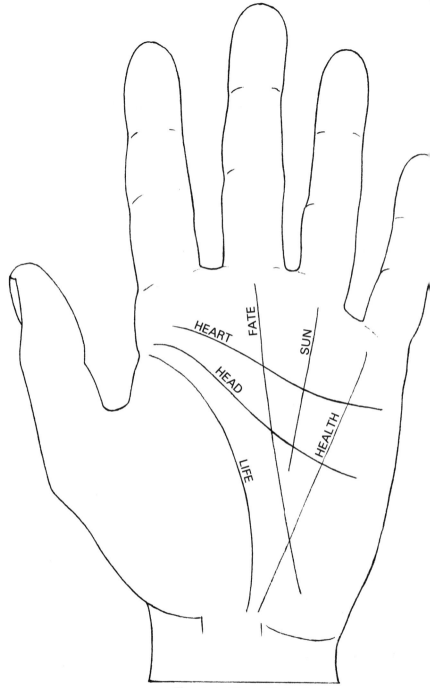

The principal lines of the hand.

THE LINES

Every line on your palm is of importance, but here are six lines which appear on most people's hands.

Heart Line
This represents your attitude and approach to matters of love and your sex drive. A strong heart line suggests excellent relationships with the opposite sex.

Head Line
A person with a prominent head line is a born leader. A strong imagination will be in evidence.

Life Line
This signifies your business abilities and achievements. If prominent, your ambitions will be important—you'll want to get ahead as quickly as possible.

Fate Line
This is almost solely connected with everyday work or a career and how successful one would be depending on one's personal efforts. The more prominent the line, the more success is indicated.

Health Line
A long health line can be taken as a good sign and indicates that you'll have very little illness. If it is broken, ill health can be expected at some point in life.

Sun Line
If strong, you'll have a magnetic personality and always be surrounded by friends. Your enemies will be few. Your personality will assist you to overcome many problems.

I always look for initials on either side of the life line. These can indicate the name of a partner or someone prominent in the subject's life. Some people have a double lifeline. These folk are usually born under the sign of Pisces, an astrological characteristic of which is that a subject may live one life while acting out another.

Chapter 13
A TEACUP TELLS ALL

THE ORIGIN of teacup reading is vague, but it is known to have been practised in China before the habit of drinking tea spread to other parts of the world.

Studying the arrangement of tea leaves is the simplest method of divination. There is no need for textbooks. A reading can be set up at a moment's notice. Nor is there any cause to be frustrated by the modern tea bag. Just burst the bag and remove it. Then carry on as though it had never existed.

We all possess some psychic qualities, and the more psychic the person who makes the prediction, the more accurate and reliable the reading will be. The secret lies in recognising what you see in the cup, and if you concentrate hard, with practice you will always see something, and that something will be that bit more than anyone else can see.

I was a teenager when my mother first taught me to read cups. It was great fun as all the family eventually became involved and we would end up as interested in everyone else's future as in our own. Many of the events forecast came true. My daughter Selina has never drunk tea in her life, but that has not stopped her reading teacups and even when she was very young she would come up with predictions which proved to be accurate.

To set the scene. . . . Usually I like to put a client at ease, but when reading a teacup you can, if you want, look sinister without overdoing it. It makes the subject sit up with anticipation and can help to get you in the right frame of mind to concentrate.

193

When the subject has drunk as much of the tea from the cup as possible, tell him or her to take the cup in the left hand and swirl the remains round three times towards the heart. The cup should then be placed upside down on the saucer—this drains any remaining liquid away. Then take the cup in your own hands to study the pattern that is left. A plain white cup, preferably shallow, is best.

If a trace of the liquid remains you can forecast tears before the week is out. If there is none, good news will come suddenly.

As for the leaves themselves, they can make thousands of shapes, patterns and formations. At first concentrate on the individual shapes and see what you make of them. It is hard work, but once you have recognised one shape, your psychic powers will begin to work and others should follow. Look elsewhere in the cup for clues as to what a particular shape could mean. For example, if you see a number seven (numbers usually represent time, i.e. seven days, seven weeks, etc.) look out for another shape that you recognise. If you find a ring near the seven, a wedding will take place within a seven, i.e. within seven days or weeks or months.

When formations are towards the top of the cup, a predicted event will occur soon. If they are at the bottom, months or even years may elapse before it happens. Look out for initials. They can give a clue to the identification of the person most closely concerned.

It is possible to build up a picture of a person's future piece by piece from a teacup reading. It has worked for me as accurately as any of the other methods I use. These are my interpretations of the main shapes that I tend to find.

Acorn
A pregnancy. If there is an initial nearby this could be an indication of the identity of the person involved.

Aircraft
A journey will be taken unexpectedly. This could be for good or bad but you will know this beforehand.

Almond
This signifies purity and represents someone born under the sign of Virgo who will enter your life and show you the quickest way to achieve your goals.

Anchor
Changes in your career will work to your advantage, although there could be problems initially.

Angel
News may reach you of someone who is very ill and some of your time may have to be given up to looking after this person.

Anvil
You will hear of a forthcoming marriage that will cause much discussion. No one will expect it to work, but it will. The woman involved in the partnership will turn out to be a tower of strength.

Apple
Your wishes will materialise, especially if this involves someone of the opposite sex. You could also receive a tempting offer which will be hard to refuse.

Archway
An enemy will hold out the hand of friendship and help you in every way possible to overcome your problems. A permanent relationship could be formed.

Arrow
Career prospects will improve, probably after receiving a telephone call or letter. This sign is also good for all financial transactions.

Axe
Restrictions recently placed on you will be removed, but be wary of a two-faced woman who enters your life at this time.

Balloon
Be wary of overconfidence. Your future will look so rosy that there is a tendency for you to take risks that could eventually result in losses.

Banner
A victory, not so much over someone, but over circumstances that have been causing you problems. A very distinguished person will enter your life who will help you financially and emotionally.

Basket
Look forward to unexpected good fortune and if you act on information received, you'll most certainly benefit financially.

Bat
Delay making new plans at present. Think more about your intentions and you will see the pitfalls that you otherwise would have missed. There is a possibility you will be troubled by nightmares around this time.

Bayonet
Be careful of accidents. You could cause injury to yourself or someone close through haste.

Bear
An older person who is waiting to help you will comfort and assist you in understanding your problems.

Beaver
You will receive cooperation from others regarding an idea. Don't try to do things on your own, this is the time for team work.

Bees
You will become involved in a legal matter and your signature will be required on a document. The outcome will eventually be to your advantage.

Beetle
Your luck is in where money is concerned and a small gamble could pay off handsomely.

Bell
If at the top of your cup, you will receive some very welcome news which will cause a dramatic change in your affairs. If at the bottom, unpleasant news will come by mail.

Bellows
A secret admirer will give you an invitation and this could result in a permanent relationship being formed. A recent disappointment will prove to be a blessing in disguise.

Bird
If the bird is flying, there will be some unexpected news. If it is perched on the branch of a tree, plans already made may have to be scrapped.

Bird's nest
You will have more security in the very near future due to a member of the family who changes his or her mind. Welcome news regarding a child will reach you.

Bluebell
Someone close genuinely cares for you and you shouldn't listen to gossip spread by others.

Boat
You will benefit materially by someone else's actions although, if this is to happen, you may have to change plans.

Bomb
Trouble on the domestic scene could affect your work and you may find that superiors are less than understanding.

Book
If the book is closed, a relationship will break up. If it is open, you will begin to understand a loved one more and your relationship will go from strength to strength.

Bridle
You will be forced to take on more responsibility, but this loss of freedom is only temporary so don't do anything on impulse.

Buckle
You will be forced to defend yourself against someone who challenges your actions and if an agreement is reached, a partnership could be formed.

Bull
Matters close to your heart will begin to show promise and, suddenly, problems that existed will simply disappear.

Butterfly
You'll be accused of being a flirt and this could result in arguments taking place with a member of your immediate family.

Cabbage
This is the time to change direction. Your ideas seem to lack imagination and your over-cautious attitude will get you nowhere. News will come to you of someone adopting a child.

Cactus
This is the time for courage and perseverance. You know what you want and how to get it, so don't give in to other people's demands.

Cake

If at the bottom of the cup you will be invited to a celebration. If near the rim, it could be you who is doing the entertaining.

Camel

Someone who lives in another part of the country will disappoint you, but don't be tempted to seek revenge.

Candelabra

A musically minded person who enters your life will attract you romantically. This person could also solve a problem that has been causing you anxiety for a long time.

Candle

A new friend will give you a fresh lease of life and show you how to enjoy yourself to the full.

Cannon

Someone in uniform will call at your home. This could result in you being worried, but a friend will come to your aid and stop you from panicking.

Canoe

You can expect trouble with your love-life when you decide to seek more excitement. Be wary—you may get more than you bargained for.

Cap

Be careful when you are dealing with a member of the opposite sex as his or her motives may not be as honourable as you think.

Carnation

You will dream about someone who has recently died and for whom you had the greatest admiration. Afterwards, you will feel very close to this person.

Carousel

You may have to intervene when an argument breaks out between two friends who are having marital problems. Use all the discretion at your disposal.

Castanets
Someone will give you the opportunity to travel. Before you go, however, make sure there are no strings attached.

Chain
If the chain is broken, you could lose something of value; if unbroken, your career prospects will improve.

Chariot
You'll be full of confidence when someone comes to you with a money-making idea. You could also hear about the sudden death of a neighbour.

Cherry
This is the symbol of love and luck, but it's more than likely that you'll become involved in a secret love affair.

Chessmen
There could be troubles ahead but if you plan for the long term they will be overcome. Forget about short term projects.

Christmas tree
Emotionally, better days are coming and someone could present you with a gift which will speak from the heart.

Chrysanthemum
You will receive news of a friend who is very ill and there will be much anxiety as to whether he or she will recover or not.

Church
Someone else's misfortune could work to your advantage and this is liable to come about unexpectedly.

Claw
Be careful of what you say to someone you know is an enemy. They'll note your remarks and use them against you.

Cliff
Don't jump to conclusions or you'll make mistakes which could prove embarrassing.

Clock
You are wasting time on worthless projects, so now is the time to reassess your position and aims.

Clover
You'll eventually prosper in life and achieve your ambitions. If it is a four-leafed clover, it will be very soon.

Clown
An invitation will come which will be very enjoyable, but don't trust the other person involved completely as he or she could deceive you.

Comet
Something which happens suddenly will bring about unexpected changes in your life.

Compass
You are at a crossroads and a change of direction now will benefit you in the future.

Crescent moon
You will welcome the guidance given to you by a friend, but you will get what you want only if you follow this advice.

Crocus
A time of new beginnings, especially in love. A rival or enemy could make you a long overdue apology.

Cross
You will have to make some sacrifices if you are to make headway with an idea.

Crow
This signifies ill health, but not necessarily for yourself. It could be a near relative.

Crown
Your talents will at last be recognised and this will probably come about through a mistake made by someone else.

Cuckoo
A very jealous person will try to deceive you, but this is something you probably know about already so take the necessary steps.

Cupid
An unexpected invitation could involve you in a romantic relationship.

Curlew
Be careful of what you say to others or they could misinterpret your remarks.

Daffodils
A member of the opposite sex thinks more of himself or herself than you do and if you let them have their way there will be chaos as well as excitement.

Dagger
Don't trust anyone too much, even friends. Keep secrets to yourself.

Daisy
Information you receive will solve a mystery involving a friend.

Deer
This is a good omen and you'll emerge victorious over someone with whom you constantly disagree.

Devil
Don't let anyone place temptation in front of you as they appear to be looking after their own interests, at your expense.

Dice
If involved in gambling or discussions about money, things should work out beneficially.

Diver

Changes you are about to make may not only be unnecessary but they could also be dangerous, so be very careful.

Dog

A friend will come to your assistance and give you some of the best advice you have ever had.

Dolphin

Thanks to others, you'll easily face an emergency that arrives unexpectedly. You'll also receive some very exciting news regarding children.

Donkey

Have more confidence in yourself. Decisions recently made will prove to have been absolutely correct.

Dove

This means peace and happiness and your wishes will be fulfilled. Good news will reach you about the health of a close friend.

Dragon

Dramatic changes to your life will occur through the actions of others, but the outcome will be favourable.

Dragonfly

A dragonfly in the teacup is not a good omen and you can expect bad news about the health of someone you know well.

Dress

A dress or other item of clothing on its own signifies that someone will leave your scene and take up residence elsewhere.

Drum

A secret admirer will give you an invitation. Others may try to set you against this person but you shouldn't listen to gossip.

Duck
A reliable friend will give you some very sound advice regarding your financial position.

Eagle
This is an excellent figure to see and means that someone of influence will be impressed by your efforts and you'll reap the proper reward.

Ear
Although news you hear will be shocking it will also be interesting and could solve a mystery.

Eel
A secret enemy will come out into the open and criticise something you have done.

Egg
An unexpected letter you receive will give you the opportunity to make some extra cash. Someone will come to you suddenly with news of an unwanted pregnancy.

Elephant
If you are prepared to make small sacrifices now, it will pay dividends later. You'll also have discussions about a new partnership. This could be either business or pleasure.

Ewe
Much indecision will surround your life so don't do anything on impulse or for the sake of peace.

Eye
Your future could be in the hands of others but you could be deceived, so it will be up to you to separate what is good or bad for you.

Face
Attempt to match this up with someone you know and you will hear news about that person. The expression on the face itself will tell you whether this is good or bad news.

Falcon
An important and influential person will help you to achieve your ambitions but you must be prepared to be guided by them.

Fan
Someone will flirt with you but don't take too seriously all the promises they make, at least not until you know your own feelings.

Fence
Obligations and responsibilities that, up until now, you have refused to accept will have to be faced.

Fern
You'll visit a new place for the first time and could fall head over heels for a member of the opposite sex.

Ferret
A very cunning person is manoeuvring you into a position which could cause you great embarrassment.

Ferryboat
You will hear news about or meet someone who went out of your life years ago and much reminiscing will take place.

Fig tree
You'll be overjoyed about something that occurs on the domestic scene and the eventual outcome could be a celebration.

File
A metal file is an indication that it's time to reorganise your budget as you appear to be wasting your money needlessly.

Fir tree

A lovely gift will come to you soon but you may never know who sent it.

Fire

Unexpected news is on its way, but when it reaches you, think before you act.

Fish

A fish in the teacup can only mean one thing—good luck, but particularly in personal relationships which should show a dramatic improvement.

Fist

A clenched fist means that someone is trying to guide you, but you won't listen. The person will be a close friend.

Flag

You'll be forced to stand up for something you believe in and publicly air your views.

Flowers

An invitation you receive, and accept, will turn out better than you dreamed possible.

Font

You'll be speechless when you hear news of a birth, but try to keep your feelings to yourself.

Fountain

Be optimistic about the future as joy, happiness and satisfaction are on their way.

Fox

This is a time for care when signing papers, especially if they involve financial transactions.

Frog

Seek professional advice when you receive a tempting offer. When a frog is in the teacup, nothing should be left to chance.

Gallows
It's time to think again as you appear to be going in the wrong direction and for the wrong reasons.

Garden
If you see what appears to be a garden in the teacup, you can expect a new love affair which could eventually lead to marriage.

Geese
Someone will enter your home who makes a nuisance of themselves and you may have to ask them tactfully to leave.

Gladioli
You'll be suspicious when you receive an unusual request and you should think carefully before making a decision.

Gnome
An odd but pleasant character whom you meet will be full of ideas that can only help you.

Golf club
You'll hear a story about, or receive news from, someone involved in the game of golf.

Gondola
This highlights romance and travel and signifies that an exciting period is about to begin.

Grapes
Don't get carried away by a smooth-talking individual who enters your life. Enjoy yourself, but don't go to extremes.

Greyhound
Although favourable for all material matters, it may be time to take a look at your eating habits or your health could suffer in the near future.

Guitar
You'll go looking for adventure and be pleasantly surprised at what turns up.

Gun

Accusations will come from many quarters about your recent behaviour, but don't accept unjust criticism.

Hammer

You'll show great strength when you receive a challenge and a friend or colleague will eventually make an apology.

Hammock

An opportunity to get away from it all will come your way and you'll thoroughly enjoy yourself in the most unusual surroundings.

Hand

This is a symbol of help that is there for the asking but you will have to make the first move.

Harp

A sign of unity. A love relationship will go from strength to strength.

Hat

Your intended plans will work out successfully, even to the point that mistakes you make turn to your advantage.

Heart

If upright, you will display strong desires for someone of the opposite sex or vice versa. If upside down, you can expect a clash of personalities that could lead to disharmony.

Heather

This is a good sign for all financial transactions and also means the start of a lucky run.

Hedgehog

Don't hide your feelings. Speak your mind and say what you think and you'll be happy with the response you receive.

Helmet
Someone will try to restrict you and make demands that you think are unreasonable.

Hen
You will receive what you think is valuable information but don't act on it—it will turn out to be completely useless.

Holly
Events that happen around this time could prove to be a turning point in your life and you'll be at a crossroads that you thought would never be reached.

Horn
News that you have been patiently waiting for will arrive and it will be much better than you dared to think possible.

Horse
You have a faithful and loyal friend who will help you in every way possible.

Horseshoe
You will visit an unusual place and attract good luck. There is also a hint of romance.

House
Certain aspects of your life which have been unsatisfactory until now will change in your favour. If a number is next to the house, this will give an indication of when it will take place.

Iris
Upsetting news is on its way about a member of the family.

Iron
It's time to smooth out any differences of opinion and create a better atmosphere all round on the domestic scene.

Ivy

This is an unlucky omen and usually means a loss of some kind due to trusting someone too much.

Jackdaw

A burglary is likely at your home. Extra care should be taken to prevent this.

Jester

Someone will come into your life whose foolish attitude conceals the intelligent side to his or her character, so don't place too much faith on first impressions.

Judge

News about a court will come very soon. Also, an important decision you make will have far-reaching effects.

Lemon

Be wary of a colleague who bears you a grudge, as he or she will go looking for revenge.

Leopard

Don't try to change your partner in life as you are attempting the impossible.

Lighthouse

This signifies danger. Be on the lookout for accidents caused through your own carelessness.

Lines

If these are unbroken—good. But there could be trouble if they are broken.

Lion

This represents someone in your circle who could upset your plans and cause all kinds of confusion.

Lobster

You'll be surprised at the progress you make with an idea and unexpected gains will come much quicker than you thought.

Luggage
This indicates all-round changes. It also means that a hasty journey may have to be made in order to assist someone.

Magnolia
You'll be told some news of an old lover, but it won't be in your best interests to get involved again.

Mansion
Career matters will take a turn for the better and superiors will be of great help to you at this time.

Map
A long journey is possible and the place you visit will be somewhere you have never been before.

Maple leaf
News regarding Canada will come unexpectedly and you will have mixed feelings about this.

Marigold
Someone you admire a lot will snub you. Don't take it to heart, they appear to have problems at present.

Medal
Your past efforts will now bear fruit and you'll receive the reward that you fully deserve.

Monkey
Someone will try to undermine your confidence intentionally, so that he or she can benefit from your indecision.

Mouse
Face up to your responsibilities now. It's the only way to overcome your problems.

Nail
A minor ailment you suffer from should be attended to straight away or it could lead to complications later.

Necklace

An engagement will be announced which will come as a complete surprise to everyone in your social circle.

Net

Problems you have just now will seem impossible to overcome, but a newcomer you are introduced to will offer you some very useful advice.

Nurse

A relative or close friend will suddenly fall ill and this may cause you to visit a hospital. However, the illness may not be as serious as first thought.

Oak tree or oak leaf

You will prosper through inheritance. This will not amount to much but it will nevertheless be very welcome.

Oar

You appear to be heading in the wrong direction with your plans. This is the time to change course before it is too late to turn back.

Octopus

You may have to accept responsibilities which go against the grain. These will only be temporary and you'll benefit from the experience.

Orchid

You will be tempted to get involved in a love relationship that is taboo. If care isn't taken, this could lead to arguments and an embarrassing situation.

Otter

You'll be delighted at news you receive of a young person and this will prove that remarks you made in the past were absolutely correct.

Padlock

Ties or restrictions will be placed on you by a member of the family, but don't allow this to occur without a fight.

Pagoda
A place you visit for the first time will give you an idea of how to make extra money. If you put enough thought into this, it will be successful.

Palm tree
Someone in your immediate circle wants to be linked with you romantically and this person could have more to offer you than you realise.

Panther
A big disappointment may force you to change plans. A friend has let you down and you may never trust them again.

Parachute
This is lucky and you will learn something at the last minute that will stop you from making a big mistake.

Parrot
Although your intentions are good, be careful to whom you offer advice. What you say could be grossly mis-interpreted.

Peacock
Curb a tendency to boast about what you have achieved or jealous friends could take the sting out of your tail.

Pen
Something you have been putting off because it's distasteful should be attended to immediately.

Pig
It's time to get your priorities right or someone will make difficulties for you when they refuse to assist you any longer.

Pigeon
Surprising, but good, news will come from another country. This could mean you taking a journey in the very near future.

Pipe
Harmony will reign when someone from outside the family steps in and plays the role of peacemaker.

Policeman
You'll become involved in a legal matter which doesn't directly concern you. A visit to a courtroom may be necessary, however.

Postman
A letter you receive will be extremely important and you may have to seek advice before you take any steps.

Pyramid
This indicates vast improvements in your life and suggests that you'll achieve something which no-one thought possible.

Queen
A figure such as this represents a very important person who will guide and advise you in your career.

Question mark
This is a warning sign and means you should do nothing unless you are absolutely sure what you are getting yourself involved in.

Rabbit
A hectic social life can be looked forward to and someone who up until now has just been a friend could flatter and compliment you.

Raft
You will be stopped from making a complete fool of yourself and your rescuer will have more than a few words of wisdom to say.

Rainbow

You won't get much better than this in a teacup. It indicates excellent prospects in your career. A partner or loved one could also spring a surprise which will make you very happy.

Raven

Someone will tell you bad news which will make you very sad and a short journey may have to be made in connection with this.

Razor

You'll be involved in quarrels that are largely your own fault and if you don't apologise, a relationship could be broken off permanently.

Rocket

New opportunities will come which will put your bank balance in a healthier state. It can also mean news of a birth.

Rose

This can mean so many things, but they are all connected with happiness and prosperity. If you are single, you could receive a proposal; if married, it could be the birth of a child or an opportunity to engage in a new business venture.

Saddle

A golden opportunity will come to you which you should waste no time in accepting. If you wait, someone else could snatch it from your grasp.

Sailor

Someone from another country will contact you by mail. This letter will be important and will call for an immediate reply.

Scales

You'll be torn in two directions over a decision you have to make regarding a member of the opposite sex. Don't let others sway you from doing what you think is right.

Scissors

People close to you will be awkward and you may have to use some very hurtful words in order to get your message across.

Seagull

Trouble ahead. Now is the time to say what you think before it's too late.

Shark

Prepare yourself for trouble at work. A colleague could be lulling you into a false sense of security.

Shell

An outsider will come to you who will give you hope in connection with something that is worrying you greatly, and eventually justice will be seen to be done.

Snake

This signifies misfortune which, as a rule, is brought about by someone who is working in the background; someone who has his or her own interests at heart and no one else's.

Snowdrop

Your feelings will change for a member of the opposite sex and this eventually should lead to more brightness and excitement coming into your life.

Stag

You'll refuse certain responsibilities which could lead to arguments. You have your own life to lead, so don't let others tie you down.

Star
This is a very good omen and indicates that the health of yourself or someone very close will show a dramatic improvement.

Swallow
A move from one area to another is likely although this may only be a temporary change of residence.

Swan
Your hidden desires could become a reality, but this is likely to happen in the most unexpected way.

Table
Discussions will take place about joint money matters and it may be some time before an agreement is finally reached.

Telephone
You will receive an important telephone call which will allow you to go ahead with plans for the future.

Tiger
Others will intervene in your affairs and help you get what you want faster than you could have done on your own.

Torch
A very regal but domineering person will fight on your behalf over an injustice that has been done to you.

Umbrella
You will be protected from outside influences by someone in the household who puts himself or herself in danger in order to help you.

Vase
Others will advise you to change your mind. Listen to what they have to say and you will reap the benefit.

Volcano
Trouble will erupt from your social circle because some-one has let a secret out unintentionally.

Water lily
Someone you know well, but not romantically, will pour out his or her heart to you and you could be tempted to get involved emotionally.

Wheel
A change of heart is forecast and you'll go from one extreme to another, leaving everyone confused and bewildered by your actions.

Windmill
You will show everyone just how much ability you have when you achieve something that even you thought was impossible.

Wine glass
A very big celebration is near which you will have to attend although you may have mixed feelings about this.

Wishing well
This is a wonderful symbol and ensures that the person involved in the reading will have a wish come true.

Yacht
A surprise gift will be received, but you may have to keep this a secret as it could hurt someone else's feelings.

Chapter 14
. . . BUT DON'T JUST TAKE MY WORD FOR IT!

*D*ARLINDA *is quite the most astonishingly accurate clairvoyant I have contacted and believe me I have been in touch with a few. It's a subject that has always fascinated me. I could take up the whole book with predictions she has made, but I will quote only three.*

I had been offered what seemed like a very good job and I asked Darlinda about this; she told me that within a few days I would get an even better offer from someone I hadn't seen for a long time and who lived in Edinburgh. She actually described the way this person moved. Needless to say two days later I had a telephone call and ended up with another job.

I had been looking for a flat for what seemed like years and eventually said to Darlinda 'Will I ever find a flat?' Her reply was not yes or no but 'It will have the longest windows you have ever seen and when the sun shines it will be incredible.' I forgot all about this and several months later I was sitting in my new flat when the sun came out. I couldn't believe it. It was as though I was outside in the sunshine.

On a more sinister level, she has death warnings when she sees a black Ford Capri car. We went out to lunch one day and she said 'I'll hear of a death today; there's a black Ford Capri.' I found this highly amusing until she saw another one and this meant she would hear of two deaths that day. I got home and was told that a dear friend had died and about ten minutes later Darlinda phoned to say that another dear mutual friend had died at lunch time.

Yes, truly a remarkable lady.

KITTY LAMONT

In 1983 I had an appointment with a new buyer in my showroom who was coming to see our range for their chain of shops in Scotland. After the initial five minutes of introduction etc., Janis [Janis Sue, owner of 'Signature Boutique'] *and I found we had masses in common and we somehow got diversified from business and started talking about clairvoyants. I started raving and talking about the one I knew in London, and Janis about 'Darlinda' (who was unknown to me then). We decided that I should see Darlinda and Janis should see my clairvoyant in London! So a business visit to Glasgow was organised for me and during my lunch hour I saw Darlinda. Still, to date, I cannot forget the most wonderfully warm welcome that I received together with my astonishment (at how it was possible that Darlinda could have known so much about my past and present) and my feeling of intrigue regarding the future. I was not as experienced as today so I didn't make any notes nor did I tape my reading (I wish I had).*

Five major points remained in my mind. Four years later every single one of them happened to me, among them, expansion of my business, my ex-husband leaving his job and joining my Company, and my divorce. At the time all three predictions were absolutely impossible in my mind.

I saw Darlinda again for the second time on 13th February, 1989, and a third meeting on 20th September 1989. It's amazing again how she predicted things that one would not dream of. The powers that lie within Darlinda are unique and the comfort, hope, and positive thoughts that this amazing lady causes to blossom within one makes life more than worthwhile.

I am totally addicted to Darlinda for friendship, predictions and decision making!

NAZY COOK

Of all the many accurate predictions Darlinda has made for me there are perhaps three which stand out from the others and all of which were connected with turning points in my career. These three events were foretold by Darlinda on separate occasions—one was over the phone!—and each time I had no idea how important the events she saw would be to me.

The first was in the mid-1970's, not long after I graduated from Drama College—I was just about to start a season with the theatre–in–education company working out of Dundee Repertory Theatre. Darlinda told me she saw me standing on a wide stage, alone, wearing a long red dress and a red veil, with flowers in my hair. I was holding my hands out to the audience trying to stop the applause, but they went on cheering.

I did the theatre–in–education tour and at the end of a gruelling season I was totally exhausted and mentally at a very low ebb. I decided I had picked the wrong profession for me as I could not see where the fun was any more, and I went to work in my mum's office until I decided what to do with myself. Several weeks later Stephen MacDonald, then the artistic director of Dundee Rep., phoned me and asked if I would be interested in playing the part of Rosalind in 'As you like it' by William Shakespeare! 'Interested' was the understatement of the decade! All thoughts of another career disappeared and off I went to Dundee. To cut a long story short, there I was on the opening night, which had been a roaring success, standing alone in the middle of the stage wearing a long red dress and a red veil, with flowers in my hair! The audience were clapping and cheering and I waited for the applause to die down so that I could speak the epilogue. I waited and waited and finally I lifted my arms to ask for silence; as I did so I suddenly remembered what Darlinda had said! I never again spoke the epilogue so well as I did that night—inspiration comes from the strangest places!

Playing Rosalind was the beginning of a four year association with Stephen MacDonald, first at Dundee and then at the Royal Lyceum Theatre in Edinburgh. In those four years, right at the start of my career, I had the opportunity to play a string of roles any actress would give her eye teeth to play and which taught me more than I can say. Darlinda saw the importance of that role for me.

The second prediction was Darlinda's detailed description of the cottage I lived in when I went to Stratford to work with the Royal Shakespeare Company. At the time I thought this must be a description of the house I would live in as my permanent home as she described the rolling green countryside surrounding the cottage, and I couldn't see myself moving away from London, where most of my work is, for many years. Needless to say, joining the Royal Shakespeare Company was another major step in my career.

The third prediction, and definitely the most uncanny, came one evening when I was working with the Royal Exchange Theatre in Manchester. It was September and I had phoned home. I was chatting to mum, who mentioned that Darlinda had dropped round. More for a bit of fun than anything else I asked Darlinda to read my cards—she always has a set of Tarot cards with her! Mum and I went on chatting for a bit and then Mum said Darlinda had a message for me. She said I would win an award for acting and receive the award in a big London hotel from a member of the Royal Family. This was to happen before the end of the year! About three weeks later Marilyn Imrie, a producer with BBC radio, phoned me to say that I had been nominated for the Pye Radio Award for best performance by an actress for my performance in 'Can you hear me?' by Trisha Fine, a play we had recorded that summer. I told Marilyn not to worry, that I would win the award. I'm sure Marilyn thought I had some secret source of information within the judging panel until

I told her about Darlinda! Sure enough that November I went to the Savoy Hotel in London and was handed my award by Princess Alexandra!

The wonderful thing about Darlinda is that through all the trials and tribulations she always makes me feel that everything will come right in the end—I believe her! Wouldn't you?

MAUREEN BEATTIE